ANDREA DORIA

PICTURE HISTORY OF THE ANDREA DORIA

William H. Miller, Jr.

DOVER PUBLICATIONS, INC.
Mineola, New York

FOR SAL SCANNELLA

Dear Friend, Spirited Ocean Liner Enthusiast
Since Childhood & Enormous
Fan of the Italian Line

Bibliographical Note

Picture History of the Andrea Doria is a new work, first published by Dover Publications, Inc., in 2005.

International Standard Book Number: 0-486-43928-3

Book design by Carol Belanger Grafton

Manufactured in the United States of America
Dover Publications, Inc., 31 East 2nd Street, Mineola, N.Y. 11501

Foreword

It was the end of the summer of 1954, and I was returning to school for my final year. But there was added excitement to mark the changing season that year: Mom and Dad were sailing to Europe on the great *Independence*! All summer long, my sister, brother, and I had listened to many conversations over dinner relating to this big trip and how we would all be going to the dock to see them off. This would be my first visit to a liner and I was quite excited, certainly impressed. It would not just be seeing the grand liner and its fascinating interiors that caught my attention, but also witnessing the sailing with my own eyes.

The visit to the *Independence* and that departure from Pier 84 actually exceeded my expectations. It was absolute magic. I still vividly recall how the crew treated everyone—passengers and visitors alike—like royalty. The departure, with the high emotion of loved ones being separated and the anticipation of crossing the great Atlantic to Europe, was also unlike anything I could have imagined. From that day on, whenever I came into Manhattan with a date, it was understood that, before we went to dinner or a show, we had to visit whatever liner happened to be in port, waiting to sail to some far-off destination. I will never forget the day I visited the *Andrea Doria*. I had seen the *Queen Mary*, the *Queen Elizabeth*, the *Liberté*, and others, but upon seeing the *Doria*, with her perfect, yacht-like design, that tapered funnel, and her ideal size, I found her instantly appealing. You might say it was love at first sight! The visit onboard was as wonderful. I found her interiors to be not only very beautiful, but so advanced compared to the quiet, conservative *Independence* and other liners. And, of course, the rich charm of the Italian crew added plenty. I liked her sister ship, the *Cristoforo Colombo*, as well, but the *Doria* had the slight edge for me. She had something extra.

In the fall of 1955, after entering the steamship business, I worked for Moore-McCormack Lines in Lower Manhattan, with offices in Bowling Green. At lunchtime, I would frequent the offices of other steamship lines in search of photos and postcards of their ships. I gradually began to accumulate quite a collection. Naturally, items from the Italian Line and especially its flagship *Andrea Doria* were very high on my list of favorites.

I also remember well arriving at my office at 11 Broadway on July 26, 1956, the morning after the collision between the *Doria* and the *Stockholm*. Everyone in "Shipping Row," as we called it, seemed to be in a state of shock. How could this have possibly happened? And between two liners? Many felt it was a modern-day version of the *Titanic* story! It had all the elements—a near-unsinkable liner, an unexpected disaster, and the tragedy of the lost passengers and ship. It immediately became the big topic of conversation, and discussions continued for weeks afterward. As bold as it now sounds, I went to the Italian Line's offices on nearby State Street and actually received some especially nice photos of the *Doria*. The Italian Line, it seems, was happy to rid themselves of the pictures, since keeping them was considered bad luck. It was as if the *Andrea Doria* did not exist.

Years later, when it was time to move to a new, larger apartment in New York City, I decided that I had far too much ocean liner "stuff" and had to downsize. I took the *Doria* items, among others, to an antique show at the Park Avenue Armory and sold the lot. Like others, I felt that the great age of the ocean liner was all but over. There seemed no sense in hanging on. A few years passed before a friend, himself an avid passenger ship collector, rekindled my interest and—like the flash of a lighted flame—got me collecting again. I even contacted the Rhode Island–based dealer that had bought my *Andrea Doria* collection at the Armory and, most fortunately, was able to repurchase almost all of it. I also decided that, while collecting on many other great ships, I would concentrate on one liner, trying to obtain anything and everything on her, from A to Z. I selected the beautiful *Andrea Doria*. Fortunately, collecting liner materials was not yet as popular or as expensive, and so I was able to build a substantial collection on the Italian Line flagship. To this day, I have large models, pieces of china, tons of literature from her keel laying to her final crossing, and have even commissioned paintings of her. I also fell upon a vast collection from the Italian Line's office on Charles Street in Boston. This treasury included not only photos, but all the files from that tragic night off Nantucket, the sinking the next morning, the rescue, and the aftermath of dispositions and inquiries. As from that first visit in 1954, I am still madly in love with the *Andrea Doria*.

Interest in the *Doria* has grown tremendously over the years, partly as a result of the many recent dives to her wreckage in the western Atlantic. There have also been new books about her, television documentaries, and, in many ways, a renewed, spirited fascination with that last era of Atlantic liners. I am therefore delighted and honored to be called upon by Bill Miller to write this foreword about my favorite liner. For me, there was no ship quite like the *Andrea Doria* and, in this pictorial, she and the other great Italian liners seem to sail again.

Richard Faber
New York City
Summer 2004

ACKNOWLEDGEMENTS

Thanking everyone when writing a book is always a great task. Like other authors, I fear forgetting someone—it is akin, in ways, to a ship captain leaving passengers at the dock. There are so many kind helpers—patient souls and generous "shipmates"—who have shared information, insights, unpublished photos, vintage brochures, news clippings, and more. Each of the individuals named below became—even years after the existence of the *Andrea Doria*—"crewmembers" of the Italian Line, working to keep the memory of the ship alive.

First and foremost, my greatest respect and warmest regard for the great Dover Publications, for its integrity, continued high standards, and uninterrupted interest in such ocean liner titles. It has been a glorious twenty-five-year association for me. Special thanks to Clarence Strowbridge for taking on these projects, to Jenny Bak for her fine editorial skills, and to Carol Belanger Grafton for her exceptional photo layout.

Other first-class contributors include my dear friend Richard Faber, not only for priceless photos, invaluable printed materials, and his evocative recollections and additions, but also for his most reflective foreword. Then there is the exceptional Maurizio Eliseo, a magnificent individual, who is not only a blaze of knowledge, but of diverse skills. Unquestionably, Abe Michaelson is "Crewmember of the Year" for his tireless work of record keeping, filling orders, and dispatching books to the four corners.

Sharing the Boat Deck with them are Ernest Arroyo, Frank Braynard, Tom Cassidy, Anthony Cooke, the late Frank Cronican, the late John Gillespie, Lewis and the late Ruth Gordon, Charles Howland, Bob Kelly, Norman Knebel, Captain James McNamara, Paolo Piccione, David Rulon, Sal Scannella, Der Scutt, Captain Ed Squire, Richard Stepler, Al Tallia, and Frank Trumbour.

Other loyal and faithful assistants include Nick Arena, Captain Stephen Card, Michael Cassar, Tom Chirby, Luis Miguel Correia, Michael Dollenbacher, Frank Duffy, the late Alex Duncan, John Ferguson, Jim Flood, Captain Raffaele Gavino, Andy Hernandez, Pine Hodges, David Hutchings, Dewey and Tricia Kennell, Arnold Kludas, Peter Knego, Stanley Lehrer, Rosalbo Lottero, Victor Marinelli, Mitchell Mart, the late Vincent Messina, Hisashi Noma, Marcia Peterson, Mario Pulice, Tony Ralph, Fred Rodriguez, Richard Romano, Captain Vittorio Sartori, the late Antonio Scrimali, Dan Trachtenberg, Gordon Turner, Albert Wilhelmi, David Williams, and Alan Zamchick.

Firms and organizations that helped include Carnival Cruise Lines, Celebrity Cruises, Costa Cruises, Crystal Cruises, Cunard Line, Italian Line, Maritime Matters, Moran Towing & Transportation Company, the Ocean Liner Council at South Street Seaport Museum, Radisson-Seven Seas Cruises, Steamship Historical Society, Valtur Cruises, World Ocean & Cruise Society, and World Ship Society.

Introduction

One of the most famous ships of the twentieth century, the *Andrea Doria* and her tragic sinking on that summer morning in July 1956 has assured for her an immortal place in maritime history. She was also one of the most important transatlantic luxury liners of the immediate post–World War II era. She was certainly the most noteworthy Italian liner of the 1950s—the national "renaissance ship" that came in the wake of the destruction and devastation of the war. She was a great symbol, not only to Italian marine designers, shipbuilders and seamen, but to the nation itself. More than anything else, the building of the *Andrea Doria*—large, fast and luxurious—was a rebirth: Italy was revitalizing and, perhaps more than anything else, this ship was the greatest indication. It is therefore with both pride and delight that I have prepared this tribute, which coincidentally will be published between the fiftieth anniversaries of her completion and her end.

Writing about the *Andrea Doria* has sparked some personal memories for me. Frankie O'Connell was my grade school classmate and neighbor in Hoboken, the New Jersey waterfront city, in the 1950s. He lived in the adjoining Park Avenue brownstone. His father was a longshoreman, a "docker," who worked on the old 8th Street pier, which in those days handled the freighters of two British shipping companies, the Cunard Line and the Bristol City Line. He was occasionally reassigned to the 1st Street pier and would grab an extra day's pay with the American Export Lines. Export ships plied the mid-Atlantic run to and from the Mediterranean and Middle East. I recall the summer evening when Frankie's father came home to Park Avenue laden with gifts from an Export freighter that had just arrived from Alexandria and Genoa. There were alabaster ashtrays, alabaster vases and—to my excitement—an alabaster model of the *Andrea Doria*. It was about twelve inches long and was painted to resemble the Italian liner: black hull, white upperworks, and appropriate green, red, and white funnel colors. There was a rather crude mast atop the wheelhouse and no forward king posts or booms, but there were four little electric cranes and tiny, brightly colored discs mounted on pins to suggest the lido deck umbrellas on the aft decks. The three swimming pools were hand painted in deepest blue. For years thereafter, the flag-bedecked model had a place of honor in the O'Connell living room—atop their big, mahogany-encased Dumont television. Decades later, in August 1989, I met Frankie's mother on an Alaskan trip aboard the cruise ship *Stardancer*. By then a retired schoolteacher, she was still living in that Park Avenue brownstone, but, quite sadly for me, couldn't remember what became of that *Andrea Doria* model. Was it stashed away in some basement box or had it moved with Frankie himself, by then a businessman in Minnesota?

On that drama-filled morning of July 26, 1956, I didn't quite believe the blazing newspaper headlines or television newscaster John Tillman's eyewitness account. The *Andrea Doria* was gone. The next day, my father drove me to the nearby Weehawken palisades, high above the Hudson and just across from Luxury Liner Row. I saw for myself. I turned to my father and said to him, "Pier 84 is empty!" The *Andrea Doria* had been due that morning at that Italian Line terminal, according to the always-accurate shipping schedules in both the *New York Times* and *Herald Tribune*. Some thirteen Manhattan blocks and six piers north, the small, all-white *Stockholm* was lying on the south side of Pier 97, home of the Swedish American Line. She had sailed several days ago and was not due back in New York for another month. Never big or imposing like so many other Atlantic liners of the day, she seemed even smaller on that summer's evening than I remembered. She even seemed to be hiding. Of course, her bow was missing, the forepart badly gashed.

That September, I recall seeing an unfamiliar caller along the famed West Side piers, the twin-funnel *Conte Grande*. Normally on the Italy–South America run, she had been hurriedly reassigned by the Italian Line to New York service for two trips to fill-in for the ill-fated *Doria*. Three years later, in December 1959, on one of our Saturday afternoon walks around New York City, my grandfather and I made a special trip to Grand Central Terminal. On display, in floodlit perfection, was the gleaming, glass-encased model of the new Italian flagship, the magnificent *Leonardo da Vinci*. She was due in service in about six months, in the late spring of 1960. The placards read that she was to be a bigger, more luxurious addition to the Italian Line fleet and, therefore, the assumed replacement for the *Andrea Doria*. She was also very technologically advanced; there were suggestions of her conversion to nuclear power within five years of her maiden crossing.

Thirty years later, on a hazy July afternoon in 1989, I was in Genoa when the former *Stockholm* arrived for the first time. She seemed lonely and lifeless, however, moored at a local shipyard. Her Swedish American Line owners had sold her in 1960 to the East German government, which made her the world's first trade union cruise ship, the *Volkerfreundschaft*. Mostly, she carried workers and their families, but only with the rigid consent of their Communist Party overseers, on supposed "holiday" voyages. Her ports of call tended to be limited to the Baltic states, Leningrad, Black

Sea resorts, and occasionally on longer hauls over to Castro's Cuba. Mechanically "exhausted," she was retired from these duties in 1985. Soon afterward, Italy's Starlauro Cruises bought her with the intention of making her over as a cruising fleetmate to their infamous *Achille Lauro*. But even before a hammer was lifted or a bit of rusted paint scraped, one Genoese newspaper ran a potentially devastating headline: "Death Ship Arrives in Port!" To many Italians, even thirty or so years later, the former *Stockholm* was still the villain—the sinister ship that rammed and mortally wounded the beloved *Doria*. National pride never quite recovered.

In the spring of 2001, I traveled to Jamaica in the western Caribbean for a weeklong cruise that had a very special notation: three days on Cuba. We had an overnight in Havana and a full day at a resort called the Isle of Youth. The ship, run by Italians for mostly European tourists, who crossed the Atlantic on connecting charter flights, had as few as twenty Americans onboard, most of them booked through a Toronto-based tour agency. The ship was well-run, beautifully served, and very contemporary. Her name was *Valtur Prima*, but, in fact, she was the former *Stockholm*, heavily rebuilt and therefore defying her true age of fifty-three years. She was laid-up following the events of September 11, 2001, when international travel slumped severely. She later found new life chartered to Greek operators, Festival Cruises, who rechristened her the *Caribe* for sailings in Caribbean, as well as Mediterranean waters. After Festival collapsed in early 2004, however, she was again laid-up until sold to Lisbon-based Classic Cruises International, who sail her as the *Athena*.

Today, the wreckage of the *Andrea Doria* rests on the bottom of the western Atlantic—disintegrating, entangled in masses of lost fishing nets, and littered with debris. The ex-*Stockholm* sails on, but now as the Portuguese-owned *Athena*. Interest in those ships and their collision remains high. It is my hope that, with this book, we have another chance to examine the glorious *Andrea Doria*.

Bill Miller
Secaucus, New Jersey
Spring 2004

Contents

Picture Credits

Author's Collection: pages 20 (top), 28 (bottom), 67 (all), 72 (bottom), 73, 74, 75 (all), 76, 78, 94 (bottom), 105 (top)
Michael Cassar Collection: page 25 (top)
Costa Line: page 97 (bottom)
Costa Cruises: page 115 (bottom)
Cronican-Arroyo Collection: pages 14, 21 (all), 34 (top), 38 (top), 41 (bottom), 42 (top), 43 (top), 45, 46, 72 (top), 77 (all), 79 (all), 82 (top), 89 (top), 90, 93 (top)
Alex Duncan Collection: page 98 (top)
Maurizio Eliseo Collection: pages 3 (top), 4, 6, 11 (top and bottom), 12, 13 (all), 15 (top), 16 (all), 19 (all), 20 (bottom), 22, 25 (bottom), 27, 28 (top), 29, 30 (bottom), 31 (all), 32, 38 (bottom), 39, 40, 41 (all), 42 (bottom), 43 (bottom), 49 (bottom), 50 (all), 64, 65, 66, 70 (all), 80 (top), 82 (bottom), 85, 100, 102 (all), 106, 107, 108 (all), 110
Richard Faber Collection: pages 3 (bottom), 5 (bottom), 11 (center), 17 (all), 18 (top), 25 (bottom), 26 (all), 30 (top), 33 (all), 34 (bottom), 44, 49 (top), 83 (all), 84 (all), 96 (bottom), 103 (all), 104
Gillespie-Faber Collection: pages 89 (bottom), 91 (top), 92, 94, 95 (bottom), 98 (bottom), 111 (bottom), 113 (bottom)
Italian Line: pages 18 (bottom), 91 (bottom)
Italian Line Cruises International: page 99
Norman Knebel Collection: pages 7 (top and center), 8 (top and center)
Peter Knego Collection: pages 35 (bottom), 36
Moran Towing & Transportation Company: page 115 (top)
Paolo Piccione Collection: pages 5 (top), 8 (bottom), 96 (top), 97 (top), 109 (top), 111 (top), 112 (all), 113 (top)
Fred Rodriguez Collection: page 15 (bottom)
Victor Rollo Collection: pages 68 (all), 69 (all)
Sal Scannella Collection: pages 9, 10, 24, 47, all photographs on pages 51 to 63, 71
Antonio Scrimali Collection: pages 35 (top), 93 (bottom), 95 (top), 105 (bottom)
Gordon Turner Collection: page 101
Valtur Cruise Lines: page 80 (bottom)
Everett Viez Collection: page 7 (bottom)
Steffen Weirauch Collection: page 86
Albert Wilhelmi Collection: page 109 (bottom)
World Ship Society: page 47 (bottom)

CHAPTER ONE

The Italian Line: A Winning Combination

Unlike the Cunard Line, which dated from 1840, and the Hamburg America Line of 1856, the Italian Line ("Italia" to the Italians and to almost all other Europeans) was a comparatively late arrival on the transatlantic shipping scene. The new company officially came into being on January 2, 1932. The services of Italy's three most important passenger ship lines, Lloyd Sabaudo, NGI (Navigazione Generale Italiana), and the Cosulich Line were merged. Thereafter, they were seen as one mighty, highly competitive firm—the Italian Line—with operational headquarters based in Genoa.

The reorganization was made at the instigation of Il Duce himself, Premier Benito Mussolini. Along with the directorate at the Ministry of Marine in Rome, the Italians were facing increasingly difficult times on the slumping transatlantic trade during these peak years of the Depression. Though a million passengers had crossed in 1930, the numbers were dropping by the thousands each month, such that by 1935, there was only a total of 500,000 voyagers. Germany's Hamburg America Line would merge with its other national rival, North German Lloyd, in 1931, and Cunard would form a corporate marriage with the ailing White Star Line to create Cunard-White Star by 1934. Of course, there was yet another reason: national prestige. Mussolini and his fascist cohorts wanted the strongest possible image for Italy, especially in America's eyes. It was felt that, despite the great economic worries that loomed like dark clouds over Rome, Milan, Turin, and Genoa itself, that a strong, well coordinated Italian Line, with a fleet of fine passenger ships, would create only the most positive impression on "foreigners," as Il Duce called them. And, of course, Mussolini did not want to be outdone. He wanted Italy to compete in the ocean liner sweepstakes of the day. Between 1920 and 1930, the Germans, for example, had commissioned the sleek, near-sisters *Bremen* and *Europa,* an extremely powerful pair that would capture the prized Blue Riband for speed as well as tip the scales at 50,000 tons each. They were among the finest, most luxurious liners afloat, the first in a new generation of "floating palaces." Britain responded in 1931 with the 42,000-ton *Empress of Britain,* a grand triple-stacker that ranked as the largest and finest liner ever to serve on Canada's St. Lawrence–Quebec City run, as well as being the grandest wintertime world cruise ship. But bigger and even better ships were ahead. The French were planning a super ship, a 79,000-tonner delayed by the Depression, but which finally came into service in 1935 as the stunningly innovative *Normandie.* Not to be left out, the British, in the form of Cunard, were planning the first pair of super ships, the *Queen Mary* of 1936 and the *Queen Elizabeth* of 1940, that could run a weekly service. With a departure each week from New York as well as Southampton, such a service previously always required three liners. Italy, however, had prepared its bid in the ocean liner race as early as the late 1920s.

Mussolini was heavily prompting NGI to build its own super flagship, the 51,000-ton *Rex,* and encouraging Lloyd Sabaudo to create a wonder ship, the 48,500-ton *Conte di Savoia,* well before the official creation of the Italian Line in 1932. But it seemed far better not to have these liners as competitors within the Italian transatlantic fleet, but to sail instead as running mates. Together, so Il Duce felt, these twin behemoths would carry the Italian colors to greater triumph, success, and perhaps even greater profitability. Richard Faber, the New York–based memorabilia dealer who specializes in ocean liners, added, "Both the *Rex* and the *Conte di Savoia* were the only liners from the Mediterranean that could seriously compete with modern superliners like the *Normandie* and the *Queen Mary*. They brought Italy to the major leagues of ocean liner service."

Unquestionably, the *Rex* and *Conte di Savoia* were among the greatest liners of the 1930s. Architect Der Scutt, chairman of the Ocean Liner Council at New York's South Street Seaport Museum, appraised the two Italian queens. "The *Rex* and the *Conte di Savoia* are not to be thought of as sister ships; they were quite dissimilar on both the interior and exterior. While built by fiercely competitive shipyards in Italy [the *Rex* at Ansaldo of Genoa, the *Conte di Savoia* by Cantieri Riuniti dell'Adriatico at Monfalcone], they both exemplified enormous pride by Italians. The pairing of the stacks close together and forward with the lengthy afterdecks made them look like Italian greyhounds. Each offered grand interiors, of course, but with the *Conte di Savoia* perhaps having the edge in modernism, whereas the *Rex* clung to the traditional, particularly evident in the display of living art everywhere in the form of paintings, wood paneling and fluting, decorative metal stair rails, and carpeting. Rest assured, however, each ship exuded majestic comfort and elegance."

Externally, the *Conte di Savoia* always seems to have won the greater praise. Scutt was among her fans. "While each ship represented a sleek modern profile new to naval architecture," he remembered, "the *Conte di Savoia* had a longitudinal sleekness with, for example, more elegant promenade windows. By comparison, the *Rex* had too much clutter, like the large air grilles adjacent to the stacks. And the social deck (saloon) had out-of-scale, big, squarish windows, which were nice from the interior, but out of scale with the exterior characteristics. Also, the *Conte di Savoia*'s bridge front was streamlined and better integrated into the total design massing, whereas the *Rex* had a confusing and cluttered bridge front."

In January 1932, the new Italian Line had a fleet of twenty-two ships totaling 400,500 tons. Until the arrival that September of the brand new *Rex,* the 32,000-ton near-sisters *Augustus* and *Roma* were the company's largest and finest liners. It was, in fact, the 711-foot-long *Augustus* that introduced the Italian Line to Americans. While she left Genoa on December 28, 1931, just five days before the actual amalgamation, and then reached New York's Pier 97 on January 9, there were some changes during her two-night stay at the foot of West 57th Street. Her tall twin funnels were repainted in the new Italian Line colors: red, green, and white. Also for the first time, the new Italian Line houseflag was flown, which combined the emblems of Italy's two leading ports, Genoa and Trieste. The actual distinction of the first Atlantic sailing to New York under the new Italian Line went to the *Conte Biancamano.* Completely repainted and flying the new colors, she left Genoa on January 8, bound for New York via Villefranche, Naples, and Gibraltar. For the next eight years, until Italy entered World War II in the spring of 1940, the Italian Line enjoyed prosperity.

REX. The Italian Line came into being on January 2, 1932. Three well-known national shipping lines were thereafter grouped as one: Lloyd Sabaudo, Navigazione Generale Italiana (NGI), and the Cosulich Line (which retained some autonomy until fully consolidated into the Italian Line in 1937). The operations of much of the fleet were based at Genoa, with the exception of the Cosulich Line vessels, which continued to be managed in Trieste. Within a year, the Italian Line could advertise a worldwide liner fleet: the superliners *Rex* (her whistle seen here, ***above,*** signaling a departure from Genoa) and the *Conte di Savoia* with assistance from the *Augustus* and *Roma* on the Naples–Genoa–New York express run; the *Conte Biancamano, Conte Grande,* and later the *Augustus* to South America—Rio de Janeiro, Santos, Montevideo, and Buenos Aires; the *Duilio* and *Giulio Cesare* in a new service from Genoa to Capetown and Durban in South Africa; the *Saturnia* and *Vulcania* sailing the North Atlantic to and from Adriatic ports to New York; the *Neptunia* and *Oceania,* which also sailed to the east coast of South America; and finally, the *Conte Rosso* and *Conte Verde,* which plied the farthest Italian Line service—from Genoa out to Hong Kong and Shanghai via the Suez Canal.

ITALIAN TRIO. The great Italian passenger ships that later joined the Italian Line were already well known. In this view, ***below,*** dating from 1930, we see three large liners in port: the *Conte Biancamano* and *Conte Grande* are to the far left, with the larger *Augustus* in the center.

SISTER SHIPS. In the early 1920s, the sisters *Giulio Cesare* (left) and *Duilio,* seen here together at Genoa, ***above,*** were Italy's largest and finest liners, both owned by NGI. The *Giulio Cesare* was ordered from more experienced British shipbuilders, while her sister came from the local Ansaldo yard at Genoa. Laid down in 1913, but delayed by almost nine years owing to World War I, the *Giulio Cesare* was commissioned in the spring of 1922. The *Duilio* started her life in 1914, but was not completed until October 1923. Launched in January 1916, her construction was also soon halted owing to the war, and was not resumed until 1920. Eventually, both were very popular on the Naples–Genoa–New York express run until the arrival of the larger, faster *Roma* and *Augustus* in 1926 and 1928, respectively. [*Giulio Cesare*: Built by Swan, Hunter & Wigham Richardson Limited, Newcastle, England, 1913–22. 21,848 gross tons; 634 feet long; 76 feet wide. Steam turbines, quadruple screw. Service speed 19 knots. 2,373 passengers (243 first-class, 306 second-class, 1,824 third-class). *Duilio*: Built by Ansaldo Shipyards, Genoa, Italy, 1923. 24,281 gross tons; 635 feet long; 76 feet wide. Steam turbines, quadruple screw. Service speed 19 knots. 1,550 passengers (280 first-class, 670 second-class, 600 third-class).]

DUILIO. Soon after joining the coordinated Italian Line in 1932, the *Duilio* (shown anchored off Gibraltar in 1933, ***opposite, top***) and *Giulio Cesare* were repainted with white hulls and assigned to a new service between Genoa and South Africa. To suit this far more moderate service, their passenger berthing was soon modified, dropping to a total of 640: 170 in first class, 170 in second class, and 300 in tourist class. In 1937, the pair was transferred with the Italian government's Finmare Group to another important Italian shipowner, Lloyd Triestino, who continued to use them in African service.

While both ships were laid-up in June 1940, just as Mussolini's Italy entered World War II, they were eventually casualties as well. Beginning in 1942, they were chartered to the International Red Cross for use as hospital, evacuation, and prisoner-of-war exchange ships. With large red crosses painted along their sides and on their twin funnels, they were used mostly between Italy and east Africa. The *Duilio* was sunk first, hit during an Allied air raid on Trieste on July 10, 1944. She was salvaged in 1948 and, being beyond repair, was soon scrapped. The *Giulio Cesare* was sunk two months after her sister, on September 11, 1944, also during an Allied air raid on the port of Trieste. Supposedly, she was sunk by the U.S. Air Force when they found that the Nazis, who were then occupying parts of Italy, were using her as a troop transport while still wearing her Red Cross colors. She, too, was salvaged and then quickly broken-up in 1948.

CONTE BIANCAMANO. Lloyd Sabuado built two near-sisters in the mid-1920s that were among the grandest, most ornate Atlantic liners of their time. Once again, one came from a British shipbuilder while the other was Italian-built. The *Conte Biancamano,* shown here at Genoa, ***opposite, bottom,*** with the German liner *General von Steuben* to her left and the mighty *Rex* to the right, was commissioned in November 1925 for the Naples–Genoa–New York express run. [Built by William Beardmore & Company Limited, Glasgow, Scotland, 1925. 24,416 gross tons; 653 feet long; 76 feet wide. Steam turbines, twin screw. Service speed 20 knots. 1,750 passengers as built (280 first-class, 420 second-class, 390 third-class, 660 fourth-class).]

DVILIO

CONTE GRANDE. Seen here, ***above,*** departing from Genoa (with her near-sister *Conte Biancamano* distantly framed between the two tugboats), the *Conte Grande* was another very popular liner of the late 1920s. After joining Italian Line in 1932, she also did considerable cruising from New York to the Caribbean, as well as on longer voyages around the entire Mediterranean. [Built by Stabilimento Tecnico Shipyard, Trieste, Italy, 1927. 25,661 gross tons; 652 feet long; 78 feet wide. Steam turbines, twin screw. Service speed 19 knots. 1,718 passengers as built (578 first-class, 420 second-class, 720 third-class).]

Both the *Conte Grande* and the *Conte Biancamano* had extraordinary decor. Here we see the former's Grand Music Room, ***opposite, top,*** and the first-class verandah, ***opposite, middle,*** aboard the latter.

VULCANIA. The finest liners in the Cosulich Line fleet, integrated into the Italian Line operations beginning in January 1932, were the splendid motor liners *Saturnia* and *Vulcania*. With broad, stumpish single stacks, they tended to be flat-looking and were criticized as being less than handsome, and therefore discounted by passenger ship enthusiasts and onlookers. They were, however, two of the largest, most powerful of the then-new age of diesel-driven liners. Here we see the *Vulcania,* ***opposite, bottom,*** outbound from New York, in 1932 and still wearing her Cosulich funnel colors of red and white. Lower Manhattan is in the background, with the pyramid-topped Bank of Manhattan Building (which, at the time, was the fourth-tallest office tower in the world) slightly to the left, and the incomplete Cities Service Building (then third-largest) in the center. Lower Manhattan also included "Steamship Row," the stretch of offices along downtown Broadway and side streets that housed the great lines. [Built by Cantieri Navale Triestino, Monfalcone, Italy, 1928. 23,790 gross tons; 631 feet long; 79 feet wide. Burmeister & Wain diesels, twin screw. Service speed 19 knots. 2,196 passengers as built (279 first-class, 257 second-class, 310 third-class, 1,350 fourth-class).]

SATURNIA. Both the *Saturnia* and *Vulcania* were also noted for their rich, extravagant interiors. Here we see the Smoking Room, ***opposite, top,*** and the bedroom of a first-class suite, ***opposite, middle,*** aboard the *Saturnia*. [Built by Cantieri Navale Triestino, Monfalcone, Italy, 1927. 23,940 gross tons; 632 feet long; 79 feet wide. Burmeister & Wain diesels, twin screw. Service speed 19 knots. 2,197 passengers (279 first-class, 257 second-class, 309 third-class, 1,352 fourth-class).]

ROMA. Prior to the superliners *Rex* and *Conte di Savoia,* both completed in 1932, Italy's largest, fastest, and finest liners were the near-sisters *Roma* and *Augustus*. At over 32,000 tons each, they were the biggest liners to yet sail the Mediterranean route. Built for NGI, the *Roma* came first, in September 1926, with the *Augustus* following fourteen months later, in November 1927. Heightened spirits in that period had encouraged the French to add the luxuriously innovative, 43,000-ton *Ile de France,* the Germans to plan no less than two 50,000-tonners for 1929, and Canadian Pacific to lay plans for a 42,000-tonner—the largest liner ever intended for the North Atlantic route to the St. Lawrence. Also, well ahead of the devastating Wall Street Crash of October 1929, the Italians, French, and British were making preliminary but definite plans for superliners—ships of 50,000 tons and more, and with unheard-of speed capabilities. Competition amongst Atlantic liners, their owners, and especially their governments was bubbling in the latter 1920s. By the '30s, it all came to a full boil.

The *Roma* is seen here in a Genoa shipyard undergoing her annual repairs and refit, ***opposite, bottom.*** Though similar to the *Augustus* in many ways, the *Roma* had conventional steam turbine machinery, while the *Augustus* was fitted with diesels. For a time, the *Augustus* ranked as the largest motor liner in the world. During the 1930s, both ships, having been repainted with all-white hulls, were often used for cruising, both to the Caribbean, Eastern Canada, Bermuda, and to the Mediterranean, as well as on Genoa–South America passages. There were plans between 1938 and 1939 to rebuild both liners with more modern exteriors using one mast and funnel, and to re-engine them with brand new, more powerful Fiat diesels. There was also a rumor that the Italian Line would build a third superliner to join the *Rex* and *Conte di Savoia* on the prestigious express service to New York. But as the political situation in Europe deteriorated, and war subsequently declared between Britain and Nazi Germany in September 1939, all such ideas were permanently shelved. Fiat did, in fact, make five of the eight diesels planned for the rebuilt *Roma* and *Augustus,* but these were not used. Placed in storage during the war, they came to life in the late 1940s when two each went to the new liners *Giulio Cesare* and *Augustus,* and one to an Italian Line freighter. [Built by Ansaldo Shipyards, Genoa, Italy, 1926. 32,583 gross tons; 709 feet long; 82 feet wide. Steam turbines, quadruple screw. Service speed 22 knots. 1,675 passengers (375 first-class, 600 second-class, 700 third-class).]

The first-class foyer aboard the *Roma,* ***above,*** was one of her most impressive spaces. A statue of the goddess Roma oversees the hall.

When completed in the late summer of 1926, the *Roma* ranked as the first ocean liner to have a permanent outdoor pool, ***above.*** The pool and deck space around it was soon dubbed "the Lido Deck," a term inspired by the Lido in Venice and used extensively on cruise ships to this day.

REX. NGI was more than pleased with the success and performance of the 32,000-ton near-sisters *Roma* and *Augustus,* and so planned for a third ship—far larger and more powerful. The three ships could run weekly sailings from Naples and Genoa, as well as New York. The Italian government itself was enthusiastic, thinking of the positive image that an impressive new liner could make, especially on the Americans. Such a ship would also allow Italy to compete seriously with the superliners planned by the French, the British, and the Germans.

Though the ship was initially to be named *Guglielmo Marconi,* Premier Mussolini took such a great interest in the ship's creation that he suggested a rousing royal name instead: *Rex,* which also honored the ruling House of Savoy and thus appeased Italy's royalist factions. On August 1, 1931, in the presence of King Victor Emmanuel III and Queen Elena, the mighty liner was launched. There were strong rumors that Italy would even bid for the coveted Blue Riband within a year. Mussolini himself pushed for the ship's speedy completion, which led to several problems, as well as noted embarrassments to the Italians and a blemish to the new liner's inaugural. Mussolini was among those who waved the flag-bedecked, whistle-sounding liner off from Genoa on September 27, 1932. Days later, while approaching Gibraltar en route for New York, the great ship broke down. Repairs took three days, with further delays at her Manhattan pier as spare parts were rushed on the next ship from Genoa.

Here we see the *Rex* arriving in New York for the first time, ***opposite, top,*** with the midtown skyline in the background, including the newly completed Empire State Building. The three liners berthed at the Chelsea Piers are (from left) the *Belgenland* of the Red Star Line, the *President Roosevelt* of United States Lines, and the *Britannic* of the White Star Line. [Built by Ansaldo Shipyards, Genoa, Italy, 1932. 51,062 gross tons; 880 feet long; 96 feet wide. Steam turbines, quadruple screw. Service speed 28 knots. 2,358 passengers (604 first-class, 378 second-class, 410 tourist-class, 966 third-class).]

In the wake of her mechanical problems, the Blue Riband for the *Rex* had to wait. Eleven months later, in August 1933, the Italian Line flagship finally fulfilled her country's high expectations. She outpaced the *Bremen* with an average recorded speed of 28.92 knots over the German liner's average of 28.51. The *Rex*'s exact passage between Gibraltar and New York's Ambrose Light was put at 4 days, 13 hours, and 58 minutes. Never again would Italy have such a record-breaking ship. While her record stood until May 1935, when it passed to France's *Normandie,* the *Rex* is shown here, ***opposite, middle,*** arriving in Genoa for the first time with the "Nastro Azzurro," as the Italians called it, proudly flying from her aft mast.

In a photo dated August 22, 1935, Italy's maritime might is displayed with the nation's largest and fastest liner, the *Rex,* next to its biggest and most powerful warship, the *Andrea Doria,* ***opposite, bottom.***

REX

Apart from her size and record-breaking speed, the *Rex* was known as one of the most sumptuous ocean liners of the 1930s. There were seven or so very dominant new super ships then: Germany's *Bremen* and *Europa,* Britain's *Queen Mary* and *Empress of Britain,* the French *Normandie,* and, of course, the *Rex* and the second big Italian ship, the *Conte di Savoia*. The first-class restaurant aboard the *Rex,* ***above,*** done in eighteenth-century style, was not only praised as a beautiful space, but one that offered an exceptional dining experience.

“Italian Line service was just about the very finest on the Atlantic run in those days,” said Al Tallia, who worked in the company’s New York offices for four years, from 1936 until they were closed down when the Italians entered the war in the spring of 1940. “I once had dinner onboard the *Vulcania,* which was docked at Pier 92. The maitre d’ was like Herman Gorring. He was Italian, but really a true Prussian. He snapped his fingers and two or three waiters appeared and escorted you to a select table. It was all very efficient, very classic. One waiter stood behind each of us and there seemed to be tons of silverware before us. As office staff, we were of course unused to this. We did not know which fork to use so the waiters actually showed us. We were used to 35-cent blue plate specials, not eight- and ten-course dinners on luxury liners.” Captain Ed Squire, who sailed as a passenger aboard the Italian Line in the 1960s, added, “The *Rex* and the *Conte di Savoia* represented the best of Italy’s art and culture. The two ships made you feel you were in Italy even before you left the New York docks. They represented the wonders and the romance of Italy.” With the Italian Line emphasizing the outdoor and games spaces aboard its liners, there was an abundance of open deck areas onboard superliners such as the *Rex*, ***right,*** and the *Conte di Savoia*.

Sailing days on liners such as the *Rex* were high-spirited affairs: excited passengers boarding the ship, celebrities with company officials and reporters in tow, a roster of visitors that included family and friends of the departing travelers, and then the freight and provision handlers, the dockers, and the ship’s crew returning from the last of their shore leave. “On the Italian Line in the 1930s, we had the elite,” boasted Tallia. “Onboard the *Rex* and the *Conte di Savoia,* we had all the big names from the Metropolitan Opera House, for example. We had the film stars, the big name authors, and the politicians. We also carried all the big names in news reporting—the famous reporters and journalists who were covering the civil war in Spain. We also carried the cardinals and the bishops of the Catholic Church on their way to and from the Vatican. The cardinals often took the *Rex,* and they were always met at the gangway by the *comandante.*” Here, ***below,*** in a view from the maiden departure from Genoa on September 27, 1932, porters load the great trunks that so typified ocean liner travel.

"Besides having spectacular interiors and enormous elegance in her onboard service, the *Rex* ranked as the fourth largest liner in the world by the late 1930s," said Sal Scannella, an ocean liner collector who worked for the Italian Line's New York office from 1965 until 1975. "Single-handedly, she brought great prestige to the Italian maritime industry." The great liner is seen here departing from New York on August 19, 1933, ***above,*** returning to Italy after just having captured the Blue Riband from the German *Bremen*. An especially large crowd was there to see off the headline-making liner. "The Italian Line was always very punctual in the 1930s," added Tallia. "But occasionally, there were strikes, bad weather, even waiting for a delayed but very special first-class passenger. I do also remember when Mussolini himself delayed the *Rex* from sailing on time from Genoa. He was having a special guest for lunch in the ship's first-class dining room. His name—Adolf Hitler."

As the *Rex* prepares for a midnight sailing, ***opposite, top,*** note the separate gangways connecting to the ship for each class. There were also separate ones for visitors, as well as crew. "The Italian Line in the 1930s was very, very class conscious," remembered Tallia. "There were even class divisions in the New York offices—one downtown, one on Fifth Avenue, and one at Pier 92. With each promotion on shore, your privileges were extended from the tourist-class dining room to second class and finally to first class. With the first-class restaurant, you were also permitted to use the ship's store, even while in port. We were always reminded, however, that we were never to mingle with the low ends of the crew. With each promotion in the office, we were told that we had to maintain the dignity of both the Italian Line offices and our position."

CONTE DI SAVOIA. In the late 1920s, while NGI was planning for the superliner that became the *Rex,* rival Lloyd Sabaudo had similar ideas. They, too, thought of a big, luxurious liner for the demanding express run to New York, but without record-breaking speed. In fact, she would be slightly smaller than NGI's flagship. Premier Mussolini and his ministers were interested in her as well, especially when thinking of the glory she might bring to fascist Italy. By the fall of 1931, the name *Dux* was discarded in favor of *Conte Azzuro,* but this, too, was changed to *Conte di Savoia,* again honoring the ruling house of Italy. On October 28, 1931, the liner was christened by the Princess of Piedmont, the Italian equivalent of the British Princess of Wales. Maria Jose, a Belgian princess by birth, was married to Crown Prince Umberto, heir to the Italian throne. Eleven months later, in November 1932, the new liner ran her trials in the western Mediterranean and reached a very impressive top speed of 29.5 knots. On November 30, she left Genoa on her gala, high-spirited maiden voyage to the United States. But the mood changed when, some 900 miles west of America, an outlet valve below the waterline jammed and subsequently blew a very worrisome hole in the ship's hull. The brand-new liner began flooding in a matter of minutes. The potential disaster of the *Conte's* inaugural voyage inevitably brought the loss of the *Titanic* to mind. The news, while kept from the passengers, concerned the officers on the bridge, who realized that she could sink in as few as five hours. Fortunately, the ship's engineers and some crew were resourceful. One almost superhuman crewman succeeded in filling the open hole with cement. The *Conte di Savoia* was saved and, after some delay, continued on her maiden crossing.

In this view, dating from October 5, 1935, ***below,*** the *Conte di Savoia* is seen departing from New York's Pier 59, at West 19th Street. Her otherwise normal crossing made news that day when some passengers made last-minute cancellations following the start of Italy's invasion of Ethiopia. However, a new group of passengers quickly booked those spaces: Italian-Americans who were planning to join the invasion force. [Built by Cantieri Riuniti dell'Adriatico, Trieste, Italy, 1932. 48,502 gross tons; 814 feet long; 96 feet wide. Steam turbines, twin screw. Service speed 27 knots. 2,200 passengers (500 first-class, 366 second-class, 412 tourist-class, 922 third-class).]

"While the *Rex* was the flagship, the *Conte di Savoia* was the more beautiful ship," recalled Tallia. "She had better exterior looks, and more style and class to her interiors. The Colonna Hall [seen here in a 1934 photo of her first-class cabin staff, ***opposite, top***] was something very special. Every light was indirect and concealed, for example. The ceiling had the finest artwork and it, too, was lit indirectly. The mythological statues in the room were lit from behind, which made them seem surreal. For many of us, the *Conte di Savoia* was the most beautiful ship we ever saw. I visited the *Rex,* the *Queen Mary,* and the *Europa,* but none of them quite compared to her. Many of us also felt that the Italian Line had the best service and cuisine as well. Italian ships also had great warmth and personality. Many in the New York shipping business felt the same. We felt, as examples, that the French ships were too cold and the British liners too rigid."

Sal Scannella added, "The *Conte di Savoia* was a very elegant ship, known for her spectacular Sala Colonna. She could also break a speed of 27 knots and is remembered as being the first passenger ship equipped with stabilizers."

A bust of the Princess of Piedmont, the ship's sponsor, was mounted in the first-class gallery of the *Conte di Savoia, **opposite, bottom.***

The public rooms aboard the *Conte di Savoia* were more modern—more Deco—than those onboard the *Rex* and most other Italian liners of the 1930s. Here we see the first-class bar, ***above,*** and first-class vestibule, ***below.*** "Portraits of Mussolini and the king were placed throughout the ships by the late 1930s, and even in the corridors of the New York offices including those on Pier 92, the Italian Line terminal at West 52nd Street," Tallia observed. "Many of the company managers were strong Fascists. Once, I was reprimanded for appearing to be less than completely respectful to the portrait of Il Duce. My manager was somewhat lenient, however, since he felt 'Americans do not understand real politics.' I also remember having a special buffet onboard the *Conte di Savoia* at Pier 92. It was followed by the showing of the newsreel of Mussolini meeting Hitler. This was considered a very special, very important event. Special invitations were even printed."

The glass-enclosed first-class promenade was an appealing place to relax during the days at sea, ***above.***

Outdoor swimming pools that included slides and lido decks were very popular features aboard liners such as the *Conte di Savoia,* ***left.***

While well-liked, neither the *Rex* nor the *Conte di Savoia* were great financial successes. The "Sunny Southern Route," as the Italian Line called it, was still not quite as popular as the Northern route through English and French ports for many American travelers. Furthermore, there was some resentment toward the Mussolini regime, especially following his military advances in east Africa in the mid-1930s. The Italian government was not dismayed, however, believing that both liners bought great prestige and acclaim to their country, especially in the eyes of Americans. Indeed, both the *Rex* and the *Conte di Savoia* were among the high royalty of ocean liners in their day.

Famous passengers, as well as celebrity visitors, were often aboard the *Rex* and the *Conte di Savoia.* Here we see Crown Prince Umberto and Princess Maria Jose during a maiden voyage visit to the *Conte di Savoia* in November 1932, ***opposite, top.***

Another noted passenger was Eugenio Cardinal Pacelli, seen departing for New York aboard the *Conte di Savoia* in November 1936, ***opposite, bottom.*** Cardinal Pacelli became Pope Pius XII in 1939.

"The *Rex* and the *Conte di Savoia* [seen here together at Genoa, ***above***] were very special because they looked like the great ocean liners that they were, both inside and out," remarked Frank Trumbour, a major passenger ship collector and former president of the Ocean Liner Museum in New York. "Their lines were beautiful and their decor was over-the-top. They were up there in the big leagues of great design of the finest prewar liners. The Italian Line had a very romantic image. This continued after the war, but I think that romance then was more in their well-known cuisine and the warmth and humor of their all-Italian crews. While the prewar liners had the same features, they had the inward and outward beauty as well. In my opinion, the great prewar liners like the *Rex* and *Conte di Savoia* had it all!" Ocean liner collector Charles Howland added, "The *Rex* and *Conte di Savoia* were great big statements of maritime power and glamor. They were fast, beautiful, and intended to send a none-too-subtle message about Mussolini's strength and prestige on the world stage."

An Italian Line tradition on the Atlantic was having the westbound ship pass the eastbound liner. It was an exciting but brief period as two liners, often traveling at a combined speed of over 45 knots, swept past one another. In this view from the *Rex*'s aft decks, we see the *Conte di Savoia* churning by, ***below.***

REX. "In the late 1930s and even into 1940, we had many Jewish passengers coming to America on the *Rex* and *Conte di Savoia,* as well as other Italian Line passenger ships," Tallia remembered. "They were leaving Germany and other European countries, including Italy. We began carrying a rabbi onboard and kept a kosher kitchen. It was all done to very strict regulations. I also recall that in the purchasing department in New York, we paid three or four cents more per pound for kosher meat."

The Italian liners were among the very last to continue commercial service on the Atlantic after World War II had started in September 1939 between Britain and Nazi Germany. As indications of supposed Italian neutrality, the *Rex* and *Conte di Savoia* continued their scheduled sailings into the spring of 1940. "We closed down the Italian Line's New York offices in June 1940," said Tallia. "But the office manager reminded us that the war would be over by September and that we would all be called back. We were given two weeks' pay as compensation. Some of the Italians in the offices were soon shipped to Ellis Island for detention and later sent back to Italy. The offices did not reopen for many years and, as for myself, I never returned to the Italian Line."

Here we see the commercially-painted *Rex* at Pier 92 in March 1940, ***above,*** while Cunard's new *Mauretania,* docked at adjacent Pier 90, is already painted in military gray and being used for wartime trooping.

By the end of World War II in the summer of 1945, the Italian Line was in ruins. Most of the ships were damaged beyond repair, and several others were in Allied hands. The *Rex,* for example, was finished, lying capsized on her port side at Capodistria, in the Gulf of Muggia, south of Trieste, ***below.*** Inevitably, there were studies made between 1945 and 1946 of possibly salvaging the liner, but she was beyond economic repair. She was declared a complete loss, with actual scrapping beginning in 1947 and then not completed for eleven years, until 1958.

CONTE DI SAVOIA. The *Conte di Savoia* was a burnt-out shell by the war's end. She had been laid-up throughout much of the war at Malamocco, near Venice. There had been rumors that she would be rebuilt as an aircraft carrier. On September 11, 1943, she was deliberately set on fire by the Nazis to prevent her use by Allied forces. Later, the scorched remains sank in shallow water. The hulk was raised on October 16, 1945, and plans were soon drawn to restore her as a 2,500-berth, all-third-class liner for the pressing Italy–South American easy coast run. But there were many problems, including a shortage of rebuilding materials, available shipyards and, possibly most of all, a lack of funds in devastated, postwar Italy. By 1950, she was sold to scrappers and broken up at Monfalcone, ***above.***

Other Italian liners were destroyed in war as well and the remains of many were sold to the breakers in the late 1940s. The *Roma* and the *Augustus,* for example, had been taken by the Italian navy in 1940 for conversion to aircraft carriers. New high-speed, 30-knot turbines went into both ships during their conversions. The *Roma,* renamed *Aquila,* was almost ready in 1943 when she fell into Nazi hands. She was never used and incurred heavy damage during the Allied air raids on Genoa of June 20, 1944. Her wreckage was deliberately sunk by the Italian resistance on April 19, 1945. Salvaged in 1946, her hulk remained afloat for five years before it was scrapped at La Spezia in 1951. A similar fate befell the *Augustus.* She, too, became an aircraft carrier, first thought to be renamed *Falco,* but then christened *Sparviero.* She fell into Nazi hands after the Italian capitulation in September 1944, and on the 25th of that same month, she was ordered sunk to block the entrance to Genoa harbor. She, too, was salvaged in 1946, but scrapped in 1947.

CHAPTER TWO

Revival in the Late 1940s

As we sipped drinks in his richly appointed office-dayroom aboard the 70,000-ton Carnival Cruise liner *Sensation,* Captain Raffaele Gavino reminisced about his earlier days at sea, especially those with the famous Italian Line, Italy's premier shipping company. Almost amazingly, the captain, who was on the eve of his seventieth birthday, never paused in recalling a ship, a port, or an exact date. He had an exceptional recall of detail; his mind was encyclopedic.

Both his grandfather and his father had been seafarers. His father, in fact, served, with the Italian Line in the 1930s, sailing aboard such liners as the *Conte Biancamano* and *Conte Grande.* The young Gavino followed in their footsteps and attended the Naval College in his family's hometown of Genoa. He, too, had hoped to join the Italian Line, but by the time of his graduation in 1946, the company's fleet was in ruins. The war had only ended a year or so before, and Italy was still devastated. He only had to wait a year, however, after serving in small, coastal cargo vessels, before becoming a cadet on an Italian Line Liberty ship, the 7,200-ton *Tritone.*

Gavino's first passenger ship job came a few years later, in the early 1950s, when he joined the combination passenger-cargo liner *Ugolino Vivaldi,* a 9,800-ton ship then sailing on the Italy–Suez Canal–Australia immigrant and freight run. "We carried 95 passengers in first class, in very comfortable cabins," he recalled, "and then 735 in third class, a sort of postwar steerage, in dormitories erected in the cargo holds. It was packed on every trip going out to Fremantle, Melbourne, and Sydney. The steerage passengers were mostly Italians, but we also had some French, German, Yugoslavian, and Greek immigrants as well. Many had free tickets that were provided in return for five years of work in Australia before they could return free. Of course, most of them never went back."

By the mid-1950s, when the Italian Line had restored as well as rebuilt its liner fleet, Gavino became third and later second mate aboard the likes of the *Giulio Cesare,* the brand-new *Cristoforo Colombo,* and the veteran *Vulcania.* "The *Giulio Cesare* [completed in 1951] was new and very modern, and a very beautiful looking vessel. She carried regular passengers in first- and cabin-class, but also lots of immigrants in third class going to South America, to Brazil, Uruguay, and Argentina," he remembered. "The *Cristoforo Colombo* was larger and even more beautiful. She was the pride of the fleet for a time. The older, ornate *Vulcania* was actually a 'castle at sea,' with wood carvings, polished mahogany, a vestibule and a grand stairwell, and a first-class restaurant that was two decks high."

Gavino was actually aboard the *Giulio Cesare*'s sister, the *Augustus,* sailing off the coast of west Africa, just north of Dakar, and bound for South America, on that most tragic date in modern Italian maritime history: July 26, 1956. "I was second mate on watch on the bridge when the captain arrived quite suddenly to tell us that the *Andrea Doria* had been in a serious collision off the coast of New England and that she was in great danger. But he assured us that she was slowly heading for the shoreline to be grounded. But a few hours later, the captain returned and gave us the very sad news. The *Andrea Doria* had sunk. It was very, very emotional. Some officers broke down and cried. We later advised the passengers aboard the *Augustus.*"

SANTA CRUZ. The Italian Line's first postwar passenger ship was a chartered one. The *Santa Cruz,* ***above,*** shown here from the passing *Conte Grande,* was owned by the Tagus Steam Navigation Company SA, which was an arm of Finmare, the Italian government's holding company. She began sailing in Italian Line colors in 1946, carrying mostly displaced persons from the Mediterranean to ports along the east coast of South America. This continued until 1952, when, at the age of 48, she was broken up for scrap at Savona in Italy.

The *Santa Cruz* began her long career with some immediate changes. Though designed by Harland & Wolff, the famed Belfast shipbuilders, she was built instead across the Atlantic at the New York Shipbuilding Company plant in Camden, New Jersey, as Harland & Wolff was too busy. Intended to be named *Minnekadha* for the Atlantic Transport Line, flying the British flag, plans changed after she was launched on October 31, 1903. Instead, she was sold to San Francisco–based Pacific Mail Steamship Company and completed as its *Manchuria.* Beginning in June 1904, she was in regular transpacific service, sailing between San Francisco, Honolulu, Hong Kong, Shanghai, Kobe, and Yokohama. She was resold to her original Atlantic Transport owners during World War I, in 1916, and began sailing on the Atlantic between New York and London. Later, she ran New York–Hamburg sailings for the American Line and, beginning in 1923, took up intercoastal duties between New York and California via the Panama Canal for the Panama Pacific Line. She became part of the Dollar Line in 1929, was renamed *President Johnson,* and resumed transpacific service. In the hard-pressed Depression years, she was out of work and laid up at New York for nine years, beginning in 1931. She was reactivated for trooping duties in World War II, beginning with a Pacific voyage in December 1941. She was then managed by the American President Lines. This service ended with her decommissioning in January 1946. [Built by New York Shipbuilding Company, Camden, New Jersey, 1903. 13,639 gross tons as built; 600 feet long; 65 feet wide. Steam quadruple expansion engines, twin screw. Service speed 16 knots. 1,150 passengers in 1946 (350 first-class, 800 third-class).]

PRINCIPESA GIOVANNA. Another interim passenger ship used by the Italian Line after World War II was the *Principesa Giovanna.* She had been built in 1925 for Lloyd Sabaudo's Italy–South America run, but was used instead on their Australian service. A single-stacker as built, she was later altered with two funnels. She joined Italian Line in 1932 and served as an Italian troopship during World War II. Although bombed off the Italian coast on May 6, 1943 (with 54 dead and 52 missing), she managed to reach Naples, and later Trieste, for repairs. At the time of the Italian surrender in September 1943, she fled to Malta (where she is seen here on March 7, 1946, ***opposite, top***) and was promptly seized by the British, who used her for trooping and as a hospital ship. She was returned to the Italian Line in December 1946 and was renamed *San Giorgio* for pressing immigrant service from Genoa to the east coast of South America. In 1952, she was reassigned to Lloyd Triestino for their Australian service, but then was scrapped at Savona a year later. [Built by Cantieri Navale Franco Tosi, Taranto, Italy, 1923. 8,585 gross tons; 460 feet long; 59 feet wide. Steam turbines, twin screw. Service speed 13 knots. 400 all-third-class passengers.]

PAOLO TOSCANELLI. In 1940, just as Italy entered the war, six large cargo ships were ordered by the Italian Line for its South American service. Their construction was slowed, with three being launched in 1942 and the other three in 1945. None were fully completed until after the war's end in 1945, when they were redesigned with over 600 passenger berths each, a smallish, upper-deck cabin class and simple, dormitory-style third class. They were finally completed between 1947 and 1949 as the *Paolo Toscanelli* (seen here at anchor at Aden, ***opposite, bottom,*** with Lloyd Triestino's *Victoria* on the left), *Ugolino Vivaldi, Sebastiano Caboto, Marco Polo, Amerigo Vespucci,* and *Antoniotto Usodimare.* Known as the "Navigatori Class," the six ships sailed mostly from Genoa at three- and four-week intervals to the west coast of South America. They were routed from Naples, Genoa, Cannes, Barcelona, and Tenerife and then across the mid-Atlantic to La Guaira, Curacao, Cartagena, through the Panama Canal to Buenaventura (Colombia), Puna (Ecuador), Callao (Peru) and Arica, Antofogasta, and Valparaiso (all in Chile). The full voyage from Genoa to Valparaiso took thirty days. [Built by Ansaldo Shipyard, Genoa, Italy, 1942–49. 9,715 gross tons; 485 feet long; 62 feet wide. Fiat diesel, single screw. Service speed 15 knots. 620 passengers (90 cabin-class, 530 third-class).]

PAOLO TOSCANELLI

HOMECOMING: *SATURNIA* AND *VULCANIA*. After the Italians surrendered to the Allies in 1943, a number of Italian ships fled for Allied ports to escape further capture by the Nazis. The *Saturnia,* for example, was seized by the Americans on September 8th and then quickly converted into an urgently needed, high-capacity troop transport. Beginning in January 1945, further conversion turned her into a fully equipped hospital ship, a role for which she was renamed *Frances Y. Slanger,* honoring the first American nurse to die in World War II. But by that November, she reverted to trooping duties under the U.S. Army Transport Service. Decommissioned in 1946, she was laid up and might have been sold or even given to the Soviets, if President Alcide de Gasperi had not traveled to Washington to beg for the return of the former Italian liner and three others then in American hands. Fortunately, he succeeded. On December 1, 1946, the *Saturnia* was officially returned to the Italians. After thorough reconditioning, she began sailing on the express run between Naples, Genoa, Cannes, Gibraltar, and New York in April 1948. In their steady, well-booked relays, she is seen here, ***opposite, top,*** passing her running mate *Vulcania.*

The *Vulcania* had also fled Italy in 1943, was seized by the Americans, and used as a trooper. She, too, was decommissioned in 1946 and might have been sold, but was returned to the Italians on December 14, 1946. She was reconditioned and, until 1954, with the arrivals of the brand new *Andrea Doria* and *Cristoforo Colombo,* was used on the express route between Naples, Genoa, and New York. She is seen here, ***opposite, bottom,*** docked at Naples with a small part of the *Andrea Doria* visible to the left and the *Cristoforo Colombo* on the right. "The Southern route to the Mediterranean was almost completely revived in the 1950s," noted Richard Faber. "Beginning with the return of the *Saturnia* and *Vulcania,* as well as occasional peak summer season service for the *Conte Biancamano* and then with the addition [beginning in 1953] of the stunning *Andrea Doria* and *Cristoforo Colombo,* Italian Line service grew and grew in popularity. The Southern route offered much more sunshine, the Italian crew, wonderful food, and a longer trip!"

Opulent prewar decor continued in the late 1940s aboard the *Saturnia* and *Vulcania* (where we see the first-class library, ***above***). To the very end of their days with Italian Line, in the mid-1960s, they were glorious reminders of bygone travel. After World War II, however, their passenger configurations were reduced somewhat, such as aboard the *Vulcania* to 232 in first class, 262 cabin class, and 958 tourist class.

BETHLEHEM STEEL COMPANY
SHIPBUILDING

Both the *Saturnia* and *Vulcania* were unique for several reasons. They were among the very first ships to have private verandahs for their first-class cabins, as we see here, ***opposite, top,*** with the Empire State Building framed in the center following a midday sailing from New York's Pier 84 at West 44th Street. After a five-year stint on the Naples–Genoa–New York express run, both ships were transferred to one of the longest, most port-intensive of Atlantic liner services, running six-week round-trips between New York (and often Boston), Ponta Delgada in the Azores, Lisbon, Gibraltar, Palermo, Naples, Patras, Venice, and turnaround at Trieste. In reverse, they sailed from Trieste and Venice to Dubrovnik, Patras, Messina, and/or Palermo, Naples, Gibraltar, Lisbon, Halifax, and New York. Fares in the mid-1950s ranged from $405 in first class to $250 in tourist class. Another unique feature was that the Italian Line fare for the sixteen-day voyage from New York to Trieste was the same as the eight-day crossing from New York to Naples. Clever Atlantic travelers often booked the *Saturnia* and *Vulcania* because of the great value they offered. They were among the very best buys on the Atlantic.

Both ships sailed for nearly forty years and consequently were probably the most successful Italian Line passenger ships of all time. In the spring of 1965, however, they were retired—first laid up and then sold. The *Saturnia* went to breakers at La Spezia, near Genoa, in October, while the *Vulcania* found further life with another Italian passenger ship company, the Grimaldi-Siosa Lines. Repainted in all-white and renamed the *Caribia,* she was used in Europe-Caribbean service. In later years, her scope was reduced, making mostly seven-day cruises from Genoa to Cannes, Barcelona, Palma, Bizerta, Palermo, and Naples. Unfortunately, in September 1972, during high winds at Cannes, she was driven ashore onto a reef and badly damaged. Too old for expensive and extensive repairs, she was temporarily patched at Genoa and then sold to La Spezia shipbreakers. An extended saga followed. They, in turn, sold her to Spanish breakers for demolition at Barcelona. But the Spaniards then resold her to the Taiwanese, and so she set off on a long, slow voyage out to Kaohsiung. Once there, in July 1974, she sprang leaks and flooded while awaiting a berth at the scrapyard. She then had to be pumped out, refloated, and finally met the demolition crews.

CONTE BIANCAMANO. Another of the four great Italian liners to be used by the Americans during the war was the *Conte Biancamano*. She was seized by U.S. authorities while at Balboa in the Panama Canal zone in December 1941. Eventually sent to the Philadelphia Naval Shipyard, she was stripped of her prewar finery, converted to officially carry as many as 6,107 troops, and renamed USS *Hermitage*. Quickly, she was sent out to the Pacific. After May 1944, she was swung on the Atlantic troop shuttle, sailing to the likes of Liverpool, Le Havre, Southampton, and Marseilles. After further service in the Pacific in 1946, including visits to occupied Japan, the *Hermitage* was laid up at San Francisco. We see her here in June 1947 at the Bethlehem Steel Shipyard in San Francisco Bay, ***opposite, bottom.*** She was returned to the Italian Line that August and soon set sail for home waters to be restored.

The Italian Line spent $1 million restoring the *Conte Biancamano* at the Cantieri Riuniti dell'Adriatico shipyard at Monfalcone. She is shown here preparing to sail from Genoa on her postwar maiden voyage in November 1949, ***above.*** She would divide her time: half year, usually between November and April, between Naples, Genoa, Cannes, Barcelona, Lisbon, and Dakar to Rio de Janeiro, Santos, Montevideo, and Buenos Aires. For the remainder, she would sail the North Atlantic, routed between Genoa, Cannes, Naples, Palermo, Gibraltar, Halifax (westbound only), and New York. On many eastbound sailings, she called at Boston on the day after New York.

Following her postwar conversion, the *Conte Biancamano*'s accommodations, seen here at Genoa, ***above,*** were refitted for 215 first-class, 333 cabin-class, and 1,030 tourist-class passengers. Her tonnage was now listed as 23,562.

The *Conte Biancamano* lost all of her prewar, highly ornate passenger spaces and instead became a very contemporary liner. Here, in fine Italian modern, we see three of her public rooms: the first-class verandah, ***below,*** the first-class bar, ***opposite, top,*** and the cabin-class restaurant, ***opposite, bottom.*** First-class passage rates in the early 1950s for the eleven-day voyages between New York and Genoa were published at $420.

CONTE GRANDE. The *Conte Grande,* having been laid up early in the war at Santos in Brazil, was sold to the Americans in April 1942. She was then refitted as the trooper USS *Monticello* and had a listed capacity of 6,890. Like her near-sister, the former *Conte Biancamano,* which became the USS *Hermitage,* she sailed the Pacific for several years before returning to the Atlantic in 1945. Decommissioned in March 1946, she was idle for fifteen months before being returned to the Italians to undergo a very extensive refit and modernization. Her transformation exceeded that for the *Conte Biancamano* and included a reshaped bow, new funnels, and thoroughly modernized interiors. She resumed Italian Line service, sailing from Naples and Genoa to the east coast of South America, beginning in July 1949. We see her here at Genoa, ***above,*** with the Spanish-flag *Cabo de Buena Esperanza* behind her and the forward end of the *Conte Biancamano* to the far right.

TWIN SISTERS: *AUGUSTUS* AND *GIULIO CESARE.* "The *Giulio Cesare* and *Augustus* [both seen here in Genoa, with the *Argentina* of Home Lines in the forefront, ***opposite, top***] were the first two ships in the Italian government's plan to expand the postwar Italian merchant marine," noted Der Scutt. "These two identically designed motor ships served as models for design improvements in the *Andrea Doria* and *Cristoforo Colombo* [built in 1952 and 1954, respectively] and later ships. While they had distinctive profiles, they were rather 'boxy' in character when compared to the *Andrea Doria.* Perhaps the reference to 'motor ships' said it all."

"The *Giulio Cesare* and *Augustus* were lovely, medium-sized liners with very a graceful design," according to Frank Trumbour. [Built by Cantieri Riuniti dell'Adriatico, Monfalcone, Italy, 1951. 27,078 gross tons; 681 feet long; 87 feet wide. Fiat diesels, twin screw. Service speed 21 knots. 1,180 passengers (178 first-class, 288 cabin-class, 714 tourist-class).]

"Looking back in retrospect, the *Giulio Cesare* and *Augustus* were greatly overshadowed by the *Doria* and the *Colombo,*" commented Richard Faber. "Although they were similar in size, they were not quite as beautiful on the inside, nor as handsome on the outside, which included having bigger, less graceful funnels." Here we see the first-class lounge, ***opposite, middle,*** and card room, ***opposite, bottom,*** aboard the *Augustus.*

Beginning in June 1956, a month or so before the *Andrea Doria*'s sinking, the *Giulio Cesare* was moved onto the peak summer season North Atlantic route, joining the *Saturnia, Vulcania, Conte Biancamano, Andrea Doria,* and *Cristoforo Colombo* in service to New York. The flag-bedecked *Giulio Cesare* is seen here, ***above,*** on her first arrival in New York harbor on July 10, 1956. While the *Conte Grande* made a special crossing to New York in September 1956 to fill-in for the sunken *Andrea Doria,* the *Augustus* was moved onto the North American express run beginning in February 1957. However, once the *Leonardo da Vinci* was added in the summer of 1960, both the *Giulio Cesare* and the *Augustus* resumed full-time South American service. Ocean liner enthusiast Alan Zamchick recalled the *Giulio Cesare* and her sisters from their visits to Manhattan's Luxury Liner Row in the late 1950s. "These two ships were never quite given the credit to which they were due. They set a new standard for the Italian Line and were great preludes to the *Doria* and the *Colombo*. They also offered improved comfort and standards on the South American route, which were, in fact, very much like the famed North Atlantic liners."

Captain Ed Squire added, "Italian Line tried to restore its prewar image despite their loss of so many liners during the war. With the help of the U.S. government and the return of the four prewar liners, and then with Marshall Plan monies to build the *Giulio Cesare* and her sister, Italian Line was rebuilding at a much faster rate than almost all other Atlantic liner companies of that period."

"The *Augustus* [shown here in silhouette at Genoa, ***below***] and *Giulio Cesare* were postwar Italian statements of renewal after the devastation of World War II," added Charles Howland. "Their lines were ultra-modern, emphasized by sharply raked bows, rounded superstructures, and graceful, oval-shaped, tapering funnels."

In 1964, both the *Giulio Cesare* and the *Augustus* were refitted and converted to two-class ships, carrying first- and tourist-class only. Later, in December 1972, during a voyage to South America, the *Giulio Cesare* developed serious rudder problems. In place of expensive repairs, the Italian Line opted to retire the twenty-one-year-old ship and sell her to scrappers. She is shown here in the summer of 1973 being demolished off La Spezia, Italy, ***above.*** The *Cristoforo Colombo,* still trading on the declining run to New York, was hurriedly reassigned to the South American run, replacing the *Giulio Cesare* and paired with the *Augustus*. By then, the Latin American liner services were decreasing as the airlines secured more and more of their clientele.

The *Augustus* remained on the run to Rio and Buenos Aires until she was laid up at Naples in January 1976. By then, the Italian Line was ending all of its passenger services. That summer, the final crossing would sail from New York. Fortunately, the *Augustus*—escaping the scrappers—found Far Eastern buyers and was placed under the flag of the Seychelles, then Panama, and finally the Philippines. Renamed *Great Sea,* she changed names several times, beginning in 1980, to *Ocean King, Philippines, President,* and finally *Asian Princess*. While there were rumors that she would be revived as a charter cruise ship, sold to the Australian market, or used as a moored casino ship, she did little over the years other than move from anchorage to anchorage. She was, however, refitted on occasion and was redecorated in a Filipino theme. In the fall of 1999, she opened as a hotel, convention, and conference center, and housed several restaurants in Manila harbor. This nighttime photo shows her on November 26, 1999, ***below.*** Unfortunately, she was less than a success and soon closed.

In this daytime view from her port side bridge wing, ***above,*** we see the former *Augustus* at Manila in November 1999. In 2002, it was rumored that an Italian consortium wanted to buy her and return her to Genoa as part of that port's redevelopment. By then the last survivor of the post-war Italian Line fleet, the plan was to make her over as a museum, convention center, and hotel. The costs, however, which would include bringing the liner to the Mediterranean, would be considerable. By November 2003, the ex-*Augustus* was still in Manila, closed as a public facility, but used as a training center for crewmembers for modern merchant ships, including cruise liners.

CHAPTER THREE

A Renaissance Ship: The *Andrea Doria*

When I met with Maurizio Eliseo at the giant Chantiers de l'Atlantique shipyard at St. Nazaire in western France, where he was employed as a project supervisor in the building of the 148,000-ton *Queen Mary 2*, the largest liner yet created, it had been little more than fifty years since the *Andrea Doria* steamed into New York harbor for the first time. Despite the chilly, rain-filled atmosphere of that January morning in 1953, the welcome for the Italian Line ship was jubilant. There were fluttering flags, tooting horns, screeching sirens, and, of course, an escorting armada of tugs, fireboats, and ferries. Slowly, she made her way up along the Hudson and then to her berth at Pier 84, Italian Line's terminal at the foot of West 44th Street. Yes, she was a very beautiful looking ship, modern and sleek, and a tour de force on the inside of contemporary design. But more importantly, her completion signaled the triumphant return of the Italians to the prestigious, demanding, highly competitive, and always nationalistic transatlantic run. Out of the ashes of World War II, the Italian merchant marine was rebuilding. The *Doria*'s first appearance was called, by at least one newspaper, "the rebirth, the renaissance, of Italy's fleet."

In the late 1940s, when Italy had lost just about all of her passenger ships, the Italian Line desperately needed to revive their postwar liner fleet to restore Italy's place in international passenger shipping, and also build replacement tonnage. The four largest, postwar survivors had been seized and were still in American hands: the *Vulcania,* the *Frances Y. Slanger* (ex-*Saturnia*), the USS *Hermitage* (ex-*Conte Biancamano*), and the USS *Monticello* (ex-*Conte Grande*). Reports were that the *Saturnia* and *Vulcania,* no longer needed for Allied military duties, were to be sold off to the Soviets. President Alcide de Gaspari pleaded with President Harry Truman and members of the U.S. Senate for the return of the liners. Upon their agreement, he promised, in appreciation, to send the "most beautiful new ships" to America. He even succeeded in having the Allied postwar ban lifted that forbade any new Italian passenger ships to be built before 1955. Soon after those four survivors were restored, plans were laid for brand-new liners—big, fast, and very luxurious. The 27,000-ton sisters *Giulio Cesare* and *Augustus* came first, between 1951 and 1952, for the pressing South Atlantic run between Italy, Brazil, Uruguay, and Argentina. The intended pair for the all-important Northern trade to New York was to be bigger and better still.

"The *Andrea Doria* and her sister, the *Cristoforo Colombo,* introduced new concepts in design, had stylish interiors, and used the best names in Italian art and decoration," remembered Eliseo, also one of Italy's finest maritime scholars and the author of several books about ocean liners. "It was said at the time that the *Andrea Doria* was a 'ship built like an oil on canvas, with parts of the greatest artists coming together.' Some of her artwork were, in fact, inspired by the Renaissance, the great master artists, and of course she was the symbol of another renaissance, the Italian maritime renaissance of the late 1940s and '50s. Alone, she was a great symbol."

A three-class ship that could carry up to 1,248 passengers, the 23-knot *Doria* was built at Genoa, by the Ansaldo shipyard. She was launched in June 1951 and then commissioned in December 1952 for a short cruise from Genoa to the Canaries and back. "She was an outstanding ship when completed. Everyone was very pleased with her," added Eliseo. "She was, after all, the first North Atlantic liner built in Italy since the 1930s. She was also said to be very advanced. Her safety, for example, was assured, not only by the Italians, but by the Americans and the British as well. She was actually said to be one of the safest ships afloat. Safety was paramount at the time for the Italians. They wanted especially to revive their fine shipbuilding reputation from before the war. Earlier, the *Rex* and *Conte di Savoia* had been the very first ships to comply with the SOLAS [Safety Of Life At Sea] standards of 1929. The *Doria* complied with the newer standards, amended in 1948."

But the fates were cruel to the glorious, 29,000-ton *Doria.* On a foggy summer night, July 25, 1956, she was rammed off Nantucket Island by a Swedish American liner, the 12,500-ton *Stockholm.* The westbound Italian was mortally wounded. While the badly damaged Swede limped back to New York, the abandoned pride of Italy rolled over on her side and sank in the early daylight of the next morning. She was gone, over fifty souls had perished, and a long court battle over responsibility followed. It was, in fact, never settled.

"It was really a national funeral when the *Doria* was lost," remarked Eliseo. "It was like seeing the dream of postwar Italy turn into a nightmare. In Genoa, people cried in the streets, others stood weeping outside Italian Line headquarters, and badly depressed dockers even refused to load ships. Within two days, the Italian Line, attempting to revive spirits, announced their plans for the *Leonardo da Vinci.* She would be bigger, faster, more beautiful, even more gorgeous."

DORIA

"The new Italian liner *Andrea Doria* is of interesting design," reported the magazine *The Shipbuilder & Marine Engine-Builder* in its November 1951 issue. "In the construction of the vessel, extensive use has been made of prefabrication in association with electric welding, some of the assemblies having weighed as much as 27 tons. The technique of prefabrication has made much progress in Italy during the past few years." Here we see the *Doria* just prior to launching in a view from June 1951, ***opposite, top.*** [Built by Ansaldo Shipyards, Genoa, Italy, 1952. 29,093 gross tons; 700 feet long; 90 feet wide. Steam turbines, twin screw. Service speed 23 knots. 1,241 passengers (218 first-class, 320 cabin-class, 703 tourist-class).]

"In particular, the fore-body sections incorporate a good flare, terminating in a knuckle and a bulbous bow—a feature which has found considerable favor on the Continent for high-speed ships," observed *The Shipbuilder & the Marine Engine-Builder.* In this dramatic view dated June 16, 1951, ***above,*** we see the mighty bow section of what was then the largest Italian ship of any kind to be built since before World War II. The launching platform is erected and awaits the ship's sponsor, Italian Line and shipyard delegations, government officials, and other guests. Great excitement and enormous pride filled the day.

Down the ways! The *Andrea Doria* is launched on June 16, 1951, ***opposite, bottom.*** Enthusiastic cheers and loud applause rivaled with the roars and clatter as the great ship went along the ways and then hit the water for the first time. At the time of launch, the weight of the hull was 9,000 tons and the launching cradle about 1,000 tons, making for a total launching weight of 10,000 tons. The final cost of the ship was fixed at 14 million lire, of which 3.86 million was contributed by the Italian government.

It was noted in Italian Line promotional literature of the time that everything about the new *Andrea Doria*, Italy's postwar tour de force, had been thoroughly researched, well planned, and incorporated only the latest and safest elements. "The stem is well-raked and is of round-plate construction at the upper levels," read the Italian Line press releases. "The shapely, well-immersed cruiser stern allows a free flow of water to the propellers, the propeller shafts being fully enclosed in the bossings arranged to suit the stream line flow." We see the liner here, ***above,*** in the summer of 1952 while in the fitting-out berth at the Ansaldo shipyard.

Italian Line literature further noted, "The hull of the *Andrea Doria* is of the complete superstructure type and there are four continuous decks, the uppermost of which is surmounted by an impressive superstructure. The hull itself is divided into eleven watertight compartments by means of transverse watertight bulkheads extending to the main deck, with the collision bulkhead carried to the upper-deck level. The bulkheads are distributed to provide a two-compartment standard of floodability." The Italian Line notably stressed in their inaugural promotions, "Needless to say, this most costly ship is very comprehensively protected against the hazard of fire and, in accordance with modern practice, automatic sprinkler equipment is fitted throughout." In this scene, ***opposite, top,*** four cranes hover over the incomplete *Doria* like surgeons over a patient.

At 85 percent complete in this fall of 1952 view, ***opposite, bottom,*** the *Doria* begins to reveal her classic good looks. In addition to her advanced safety, contemporary design, and luxurious, art-filled interiors, much attention was also paid at this time to the ship's propulsion. Italian Line materials said, "The propulsion installation consists of two three-casing geared turbines capable of developing a combined output of more the 50,000 S.H.P., the normal output being about 35,200 S.H.P. It will thus be seen that there is a very substantial margin of power to enable the vessel to maintain an exact schedule." While maintaining a top service speed of 23 knots, it was promised that she would be the fastest liner sailing in and out of the Mediterranean. She surpassed 25 knots during her trials. A strong rival, the 29,500-ton, one-year-old *Independence* of American Export Lines had topped 26 knots during her trials in late 1950 and maintained a service speed of 23 knots. Meanwhile, for North Atlantic service, the 53,000-ton superliner *United States* was introduced into service just six months before the *Andrea Doria*. With a military-guarded secret of having some 241,000 horsepower, she had reached 39 knots on her maiden crossing, secretly hit 43 knots during her trials, and would average 33 knots during her regular crossings between New York, Le Havre, Southampton, and Bremerhaven.

ANDREA DORIA

ANDREA

"The *Andrea Doria* and her sister were yacht-like in appearance," said Richard Faber. "They were the most beautiful ships of the entire Italian Line postwar fleet. From stem to stern, they had perfect proportions." In this view at Genoa taken on December 1, 1952, ***opposite, top,*** the liner departs on her second and final set of trials. Note that her promenade and other upper-deck areas are yet unpainted.

A splendid view taken from the *Andrea Doria*'s port side bridge wing during her sea trials in the western Mediterranean in December 1952, ***opposite, bottom.***

"The *Andrea Doria* and *Cristoforo Colombo* may have been the most beautiful liners ever built," asserted Der Scutt. "The uniformity of massing, splendid proportions, and harmonious integration of parts was magnificent. The scale was right. A building can have proper or poor scale; most designers do not know the importance of scale, nor how to achieve it. The Italians do it perfect!" Final preparations are made, such as safety checks of her lifeboats (as seen in this view at Genoa, ***above***), prior to the ship's maiden voyage, a special two-week cruise to the Canary Islands from Genoa. The American Export Lines' *Independence* is just to the left.

The Italians were rightfully proud of their "renaissance ship," resplendent in sparkling paint, with raised letters spelling out her proud name, ***below.*** At the time of the maiden voyage sailing, Italian Line press material included a biography of Andrea Doria, the "father of Genoa." It read, "Born in 1466, Doria was known as the liberator of Genoa and the author of its constitution, which remained in force until the end of the City-Republic. Along with Cristoforo Colombo, he was one of the most outstanding men of his time. As admiral of the fleet, he fought the enemies of his country and drove marauding pirates from its shores. As a statesman, he led his people through the political storms and intrigues of the sixteenth century and, during his entire life, served his country's interests with unflagging zeal and genuine patriotism." Colombo died at the age of fifty-five in 1506, six years after Doria, who passed at age ninety-four.

"The exteriors of the *Doria* [seen here from the top of her mast, ***above***] and *Colombo* were further refinements of the designs of the *Giulio Cesare* and *Augustus,*" noted Charles Howland. "In my eyes, their superstructures were perfectly balanced and harmonious as any ships of any age. Their stance in the water was graceful from all angles. The idea of a pool for each of the three classes was typically Italian—generous and warmhearted."

Following her special introductory cruise to the Canaries over Christmas 1952, the *Andrea Doria* took a brief turn in a Genoa dry dock for final checks and adjustments before setting off for New York. This imposing view is dated January 7, 1953, ***opposite.***

ANDREA DORIA

Dressed in colorful flags and with harbor horns and sirens sounding in salute, ***above,*** the *Andrea Doria* left Genoa on her maiden voyage to New York on January 14, 1953. She would arrive in the United States nine days later. Fares for the maiden passage included $525 for a single with private bath in first class, $300 for a double with bath in cabin class, and $200 for one of four berths in tourist class with communal bathrooms. The crossing, while gala and celebratory in spirit, was not without its mishaps and trials, however. "Near the American coast, the liner was hit by mountainous waves that rolled her over 28 degrees and sent diners, tables, and chairs into a scrambling heap in the main dining rooms," reported the *New York Times*. "The new liner was subjected to a test so severe that twenty of her 794 passengers were injured. The officers said the *Doria* had covered the 4,737 miles from Genoa to New York at an average speed of 22.97 knots despite the storm, which forced a reduction to 18 knots at one time."

From the resumption of their postwar liner services in 1947 until the arrival of the new *Doria* and her sister in 1953, the Italian Line was represented in North America by its most serious rival and competitor, the American Export Lines. Here we see Export's main window of their offices at 39 Broadway in Lower Manhattan's shipping district, ***opposite, top.*** It has been specially themed to the maiden arrival of the *Doria* and emphasizes her lido decks, three swimming pools, and the amenity of complete air-conditioning. Beginning in 1953, Italian Line opened its own New York offices, first at 24 State Street, also in Lower Manhattan, and then at 1 Whitehall Street. There was a second Manhattan office in later years located uptown, at 53rd Street and Fifth Avenue.

"The sleek luxury liner *Andrea Doria,* her single mast and upper works alive with signal pennants, moved sedately into the harbor yesterday to receive the acclaim accorded to every new ocean queen," announced the *New York Times* on the front page of its January 24, 1953 edition. A photo accompanied the feature article. "Not even the bleak, sunless setting of the Upper Bay could chill the spirits of ocean-going and small craft masters who saluted the first new Italian liner to touch here since the war. The mariners' warm greeting was repeated formally on behalf of the city by Mayor Impellitteri. He boarded the *Andrea Doria* at Quarantine and sailed up the Hudson River to Pier 84 in company with a group of officials."

The liner was highly praised, especially for her very handsome exterior, ***below.*** Der Scutt agreed and noted, "The *Andrea Doria's* black-painted hull gave her a sleek, speedy image compared to the white-hulled *Giulio Cesare*. The *Doria's* stack had a 'hand-molded' shape, whereas the *Giulio Cesare's* funnel appeared to be a factory-shaped barrel—big, bulky, and banal."

Regarding the technical design of the *Andrea Doria,* Scutt also commented, "The main deck windows on board the *Doria* are vertically proportioned and similar to the *Conte di Savoia's,* and integrated beautifully with exterior lines. As in building architecture, sub-details and proportions must be uniform and coherent. Look at the *Giulio Cesare's* main deck windows—they are badly proportioned and distracting from uniform beauty. The *Doria* was close to perfection."

On her maiden arrival, the *Doria* arrived at Pier 84 at noon on January 23rd and remained in port for seven days before departing on a seventeen-day West Indies cruise. During her inaugural visit, the ship was the site of numerous parties for officials and members of the shipping and travel industries. On the day after her arrival, she was opened to the general public from one to five o'clock in the afternoon. Boarding fees were a dollar for adults and fifty cents for children, with proceeds going to the Travelers Aid Society. The only blemish for the new ship was spoken of quietly along the waterfront. It was said that under certain conditions, she had stability problems, that she was a fragile ship.

CHAPTER FOUR
An Italian Tour de Force: Onboard the *Andrea Doria*

"I was at Genoa, preparing to sail for New York on the *Conte Biancamano,* when we received word that our beautiful flagship, the great *Andrea Doria,* had just sunk off the east coast of the United States. The longshoremen began to cry. Some even pounded their fists on the pier-side pavement. Our sailing was delayed. It was very sad, very emotional." So recalled Captain Vittorio Sartori when speaking of July 26, 1956. The captain had spent thirty-three years with the illustrious Italian Line, in a career that began in 1950. We met during a Christmas cruise to the western Caribbean in 1994 aboard Carnival Cruise Lines' *Tropicale.* Captain Sartori, who had served in some three dozen different passenger ships, recalled his long and distinguished career from the comfort of his upper-deck office.

"My grandfather went to sea in nineteenth-century sailing ships and my grandmother was actually born at sea. The sea has always been in my veins, even if it passed my own father," noted the captain. "My mother told me that I started drawing ships at the age of three or four and that I always asked to visit the harbor at Genoa. Just after the war, in 1946, I became a deck boy on a little cargo ship that had been built in 1894."

Later, after attending the Italian Naval Academy at Leghorn and serving aboard naval ships, Sartori joined the Italian Line at its Genoa headquarters. "My first ship was the *Antonio Zotti,* the first and only oil tanker in the Italian Line fleet. I then went to the passenger ships: the *Saturnia* and *Vulcania,* the *Conte Biancamano* and *Conte Grande,* the *Giulio Cesare, Augustus,* and the *Rossini,*" he recalled. "The *Saturnia* and *Vulcania* were two of my favorites. I served in the *Vulcania* in the early 1950s when she ran our express service from Naples and Genoa to New York. We had lots of immigrants going westbound in those years. But in first- and cabin-class, she was a ship of beautiful interiors. She had an especially fine library. There were mahogany hallways, an exquisite dining room, a superb first-class lounge and a winter garden. I especially remember the tiled pool onboard the *Saturnia.* Very solid and strong, these sister ships took very well to heavy seas. On the South American run between Genoa, Rio, and Buenos Aires, we also had lots of immigrants. But we also had many first-class passengers including minor royalty. I remember a countess aboard the *Conte Grande* who spent half the year in Buenos Aires and the other half on the French Riviera. On the North Atlantic, we had the Italian film stars, the Roman cardinals, and more royalty. I remember the King of Morocco onboard the *Conte Biancamano.* He took all the first-class suites."

Captain Sartori later became staff captain of the *Leonardo da Vinci* and then master of one of the last of the Italian Line passenger ships, the 45,900-ton *Michelangelo.* Nostalgically, he concluded, "She and her sister, the *Raffaello,* were the very best ships I have ever known. They were magnificent in every way. And they were a fitting end to the great Italian Line passenger fleet."

After the debut of the *Cristoforo Colombo* in July 1954, the two Italian express liners were noted as being among the most modern luxury liners afloat and two of the very finest ships in Mediterranean service. Between 1955 and 1956, the Italian Line had five liners on the summer season run to and from New York: the *Andrea Doria, Cristoforo Colombo, Saturnia, Vulcania,* and *Conte Biancamano*. In this aerial view of Genoa, ***above,*** the two big liners are in port together on a rare occasion: the *Colombo* on the left, the *Doria* to the right. On the far left is Sitmar's *Castel Bianco,* a converted Victory ship, and Union Castle Line's *Dunnottar Castle*. On the far right, the *Conte Grande* is outbound and, in the distant background undergoing repairs in a shipyard, are the *Vulcania* (in dry dock) and the *Homeland* of Home Lines. [*Andrea Doria*: Built by Ansaldo Shipyards, Genoa, Italy, 1952. 29,093 gross tons; 700 feet long; 90 feet wide. Steam turbines, twin screw. Service speed 23 knots. 1,241 passengers (218 first-class, 320 cabin-class, 703 tourist-class)].

Double-header, ***below:*** passengers on the stern decks of the departing, New York–bound *Andrea Doria* view the brand-new *Cristoforo Colombo,* which, within minutes, will depart on her first official sailing. The date was June 1954. It was a public relations agent's dream come true: two new liners, sister ships as well, departing from their homeport at the very same time. Under a strong, midday summer sun, thousands lined the Genoa quaysides, not wanting to miss the spectacle. Out of the ruin and ashes of World War II, Italy's merchant marine was indeed being revived. During the *Andrea Doria*'s short career, similar scenes would occur, although mostly with other Italian liners in port at the same time.

"The luxury liners of the Italian Line were the big competitors, the main rivals, to the twin-funnel *Independence* and *Constitution* of the American Export Lines," recalled Richard Faber. "In the 1950s and early '60s, their ships included the likes of the sisters *Andrea Doria* and *Cristoforo Colombo,* as well as the newer, larger *Leonardo da Vinci*. My parents occasionally went on the Italian Line. But they actually found the safety drills lax compared to those on American ships. The Italians also had great passings in the Atlantic with each liner going in the opposite direction at a combined speed of some 45 knots. But my parents felt that these encounters were too close, almost on a collision course. They said that you could see the faces of the passengers and the crew on the other ship. It was all split-second, of course. A big rush, a sort of blur. Whistles sounded and everyone cheered. It was like madness in mid-afternoon, especially after a few lunchtime drinks. Those meetings of two liners were the biggest events on Italian Line crossings in those years." In this photo dated April 19, 1955, ***above,*** we see the *Doria* from the decks of the *Colombo*.

As the *Doria* sails away from the *Colombo* in a mid-ocean passing on November 21, 1954, ***opposite, bottom,*** her graceful good looks are apparent. She is exceptionally handsome, elegant, and thoroughly romantic. "The *Andrea Doria* and the *Cristoforo Colombo* were the epitome of postwar ocean liner grace and style," said Frank Trumbour. "Simply put, they were gorgeous. And while they were large vessels, they were not intimidating. Just looking at them, or at a photo of either of them, you were drawn into them. They gave you a happy feeling."

At the time of her maiden voyage, the Italian Line proudly reminded the interested public that the *Andrea Doria* contained an abundance of public space for a 1,241-passenger liner. With some exaggeration, they informed the public—especially the press and travel agents—that there were "no less than fifteen public rooms for first class, nine for cabin class, and seven for tourist class" and a outdoor swimming pool and lido deck for each class. Here we see the first-class foyer, ***above,*** filled with models in a series of photos made at Pier 84 just after the liner's maiden voyage in January 1953.

"The *Andrea Doria* interiors, while attempting to be somewhat avant-garde, was one of the first big steps away from 'traditional' decor," explained Der Scutt. "These interiors, however, were far short of the *Michelangelo* and *Raffaello* interiors which would come just a few years later. In the 1950s and '60s, American furniture designers like Ward Bennett, Florence Knoll, Charles Eames, Ludwig Mies van der Rohe, and Eero Saarinen were at the leading edge of a revolution in modern furniture design. Their influence was obvious to the Italians. The use of heavy, large-scale chairs with metal legs was the dominant theme in furniture design. Bright accent colors were prevalent. The revolution in ceiling lighting fixture design was also going on in America, and, of course, the Italians picked up on this development and with their usual flair, exaggerated the lighting on the ships."

"Prewar grandeur was supplanted with quiet, refined elegance coming on the scene as Italian postwar culture was enjoying worldwide popularity and acclaim," noted Sal Scannella. "The *Andrea Doria* and her sister symbolized the best in contemporary Italian art and design. Italian postwar high fashion was found throughout first and cabin class. The *Doria*'s interiors caused a minor sensation. In many ways, the *Doria* was the most decoratively daring postwar Atlantic liner. Many famous architects contributed to her interiors: Zoncada, Pulitzer, Ratti, and—most importantly—Gio Ponti, who considered the *Doria* his maritime masterpiece. Overall, the *Andrea Doria*'s style was a blend of dramatic, modern art and furniture with strong styling and bold themes which heralded a new, more conventional style." In this view, ***below,*** we see the first-class main lounge highlighted by a statue of Andrea Doria.

Italian Line advertising literature in the 1950s dubbed the *Doria* and the *Colombo* "the friendly ships." They wrote, as illustrated in these scenes of the first-class lounge, ***opposite,*** "You will be amazed at how easily friendships can ripen aboard these pleasure ships. Everyone just naturally relaxes in the spacious lounges, the elegant social rooms. You'll enjoy gala evenings, which call for your best bib-and-tucker. There are informal events when you may find yourself singing old favorites as part of a quartet . . . or attending the showing of a film that hasn't been released yet on land."

Under this photo of the first-class bar aboard the *Andrea Doria,* ***above,*** the Italian Line added the caption, "You'll find no trouble getting partners for bridge or canasta. And even a shy, retiring person will find himself drawn into the gay camaraderie of shipboard life."

"Unquestionably, the *Andrea Doria* was quite *moderno* on the inside," noted Richard Faber. "In actuality, I liked some of the decor, but other onboard areas were less interesting. To me, the best thing about the ship was her magnificent exterior." Here we see the writing room in first class, ***below.***

All of the Italian Line passenger ships had formal chapels and a daily church service that was well-attended during crossings, ***above.*** "My whole family crossed on the *Andrea Doria* in 1955 and then returned on the *Colombo,*" recalled traveler Marcia Peterson. "We became friendly with the American priest onboard the *Doria* and attended all of his services. The friendship held long after the voyage and, years later, he performed the marriage services for my brother and then for myself. We were booked again on the *Doria* for a return to New York in the summer of 1956. But plans changed and we switched to the next westbound on the *Colombo*. It was quite fortunate. We would have arrived at New York on the *Doria* on July 26. Of course, she never reached port on that trip. She sank off Nantucket on the morning of the 26th."

While not as activity-filled as today's modern cruise liners, nighttime fare on the *Doria* and other Italian liners always included a masquerade, ***below,*** and, as an alternate, horse racing in the lounge, ***opposite, top.*** The Italian Line assured, "On the *Andrea Doria* and *Cristoforo Colombo,* this is life beyond compare! A holiday mood pervades each evening in every lounge on both luxury ships. After a delectable dinner, you'll enjoy a cup of coffee and a cordial, the soft music of the orchestra, dancing on the glittering floor. Perhaps it will be a jolly gathering after a moonlight swim . . . or the night of the Gala Dinner . . . with the excitement of the ship's masquerade and the prizes to be awarded. Every night of your trip, you'll return to your stateroom thinking another wonderful day has sped by all too quickly."

The cuisine was a great part of the Italian Line's strong, very romantic postwar image. Company brochures read, "It is just a few short days to Europe, but the Italian Line takes you on a veritable world tour of gastronomic delights. You can start your day with a typical American or Continental breakfast . . . follow with a luncheon replete with European delicacies . . . and then enjoy a dinner composed of some of Italy's most renowned dishes. Or you may choose from a variety of exciting and savory menus offering the best of Scandinavian, German, and Mediterranean culinary art." In this tempting scene, ***opposite, bottom,*** we see the *Andrea Doria*'s midnight buffet.

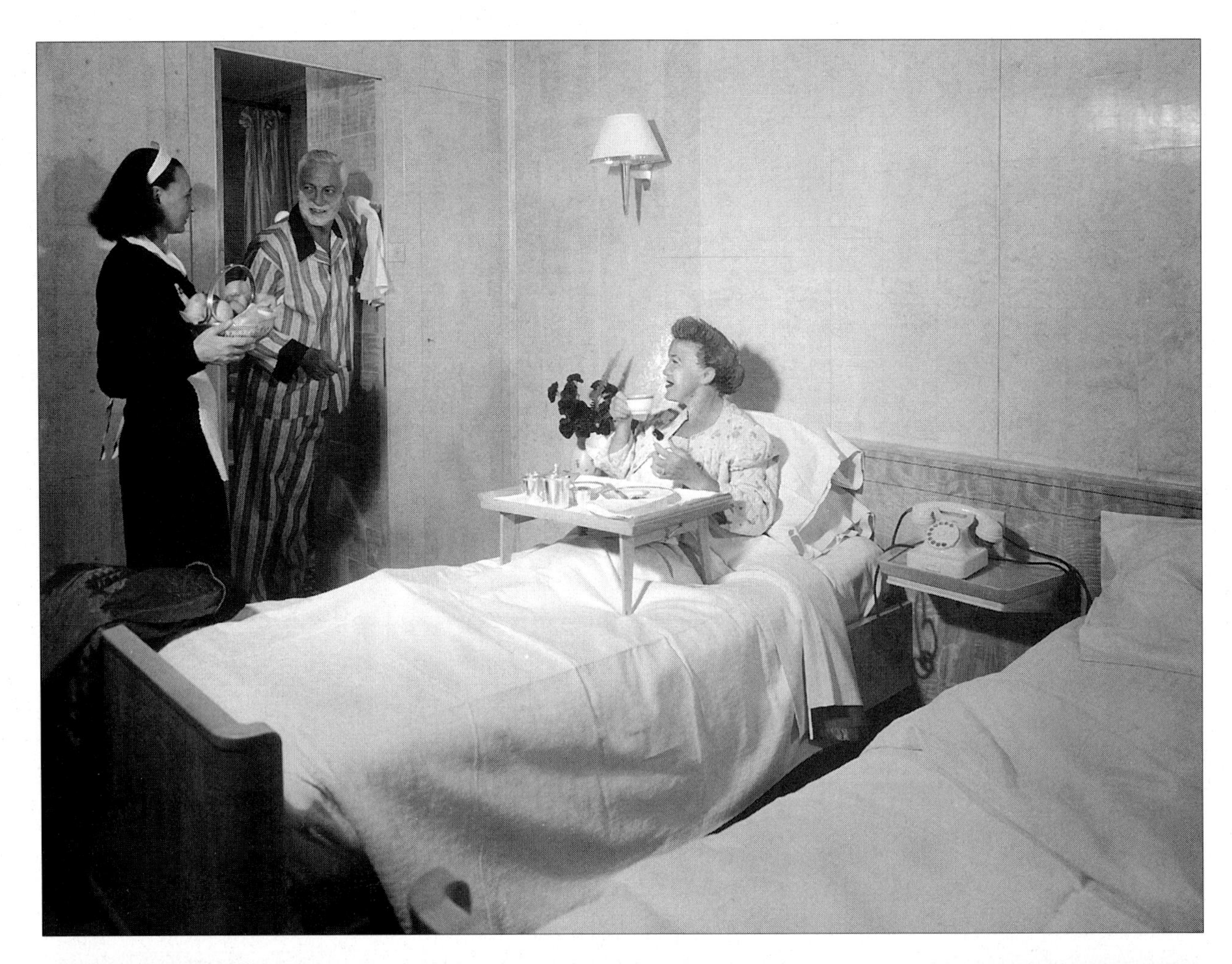

"There was indeed great romance in the Italian Line and its ships," remembered Sal Scannella, who crossed several times on the Italian Line in the 1960s and '70s. "*Arriverderci Roma, Al Di La,* or perhaps *Volare* being played by the Italian quartet as you sip Campari in an *alta moda* lounge designed by Pulitzer or Ponti. A poolside luncheon of melone con prosciutto and spaghetti alla puttanesca. The umbrellas and the sunshine of the lido as you sail the sunny southern route eastbound or westbound. Evocative aromas of pesto, garlic, espresso, linoleum polish, and sun-warmed teak decks."

"There was also the wonderful noontime signal countdown, the Carosello Napolitano crew show, the elegance, the luxurious ballrooms, the Murano chandeliers, the glorious food and impeccable service, the Italian ambiance. I could go on forever," concluded Scannella.

A sample day in first class aboard the *Andrea Doria* could begin with a full breakfast in bed. Here we see the bedroom of one of the ship's finest suites, ***opposite, top.*** Priced in 1955 at $850 per person for double occupancy for an eight-day trip to Naples, or $1,300 for single occupancy, the suite consisted of two beds, a sitting room (with a foldout bed and sofa bed), dressing room, bath, shower, toilets, and baggage room.

Fine Italian seamanship was a great selling point for the Italian Line, with passengers taken on tours of the bridge with explanations of the instruments and equipment given by the ship's officers and crew, ***above.*** Here we see Captain Pietro Calamai (left) and one of his officers on the port side bridge wing of the *Andrea Doria,* ***opposite, bottom.***

"'At your service' is a phrase you will hear time and again aboard the *Andrea Doria,*" read a descriptive booklet about the liner. 'From the Maitre d'Hotel to the Chief Cabin Steward [seen here but misspelled on the glass window as "Stewart," ***left***], from the Deck Steward and the Gift Shop Attendant, ***below,*** to the Elevator Operator and your Cabin Stewardess, all are trained in the art of service . . . and wonderful service it is! You will notice on the very first day out the personal touch that these members of the crew impart to the performance of their duty."

"Sun . . . sea . . . sky . . . and leisure hours to enjoy them to the fullest . . . that's the unique recipe for good health," declared the Italian Line. "Mild weather and sunny skies prevail even in winter on the Sunny Southern Route, making the wide, uncluttered Lido Decks a grand place to relax. And a dip in one of the beautifully-tiled outdoor pools is oh so refreshing!" Here we see the first-class pool with Captain Calamai to the right on the deck above, ***opposite, top,*** the cabin-class lido bar and pool beyond, ***opposite, middle,*** and an overhead view of the cabin-class pool, ***opposite, bottom.***

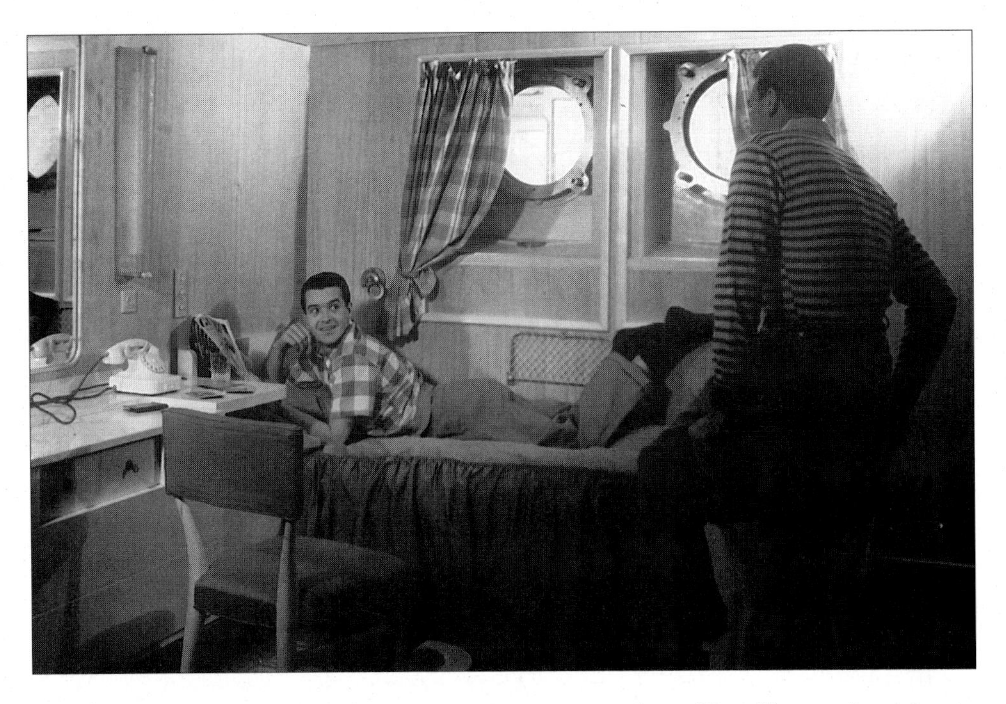

"You won't be spending much time in your stateroom . . . but still you'll appreciate its comforts and conveniences," noted an Italian Line brochure. "Individual air-conditioning controls let you select the temperature you prefer. You sleep in perfect comfort, regardless of the weather outside or the location of your cabin. Roomy chests of drawers and closets ease the problems of daily life. A perfect system of telephones allows you to talk to your fellow voyagers . . . and make arrangements for cocktails, games, or other amusements. Most first-class rooms and many cabin-class rooms have private baths. A great number of them have private showers. Every tourist-class room has basins with hot and cold running water . . . with baths and toilets located just a few steps from your door." Here we see a first-class outside double, ***above,*** and an outside single, ***below.***

Passengers in first-class suites often entertained in their spacious quarters, ***opposite, top.***

Unique to transatlantic liner companies, the Italian Line encouraged passengers, "After a sumptuous repast, you may even decide to return for a swim under the stars before you retire for the night." This is the first-class pool area, ***opposite, bottom.***

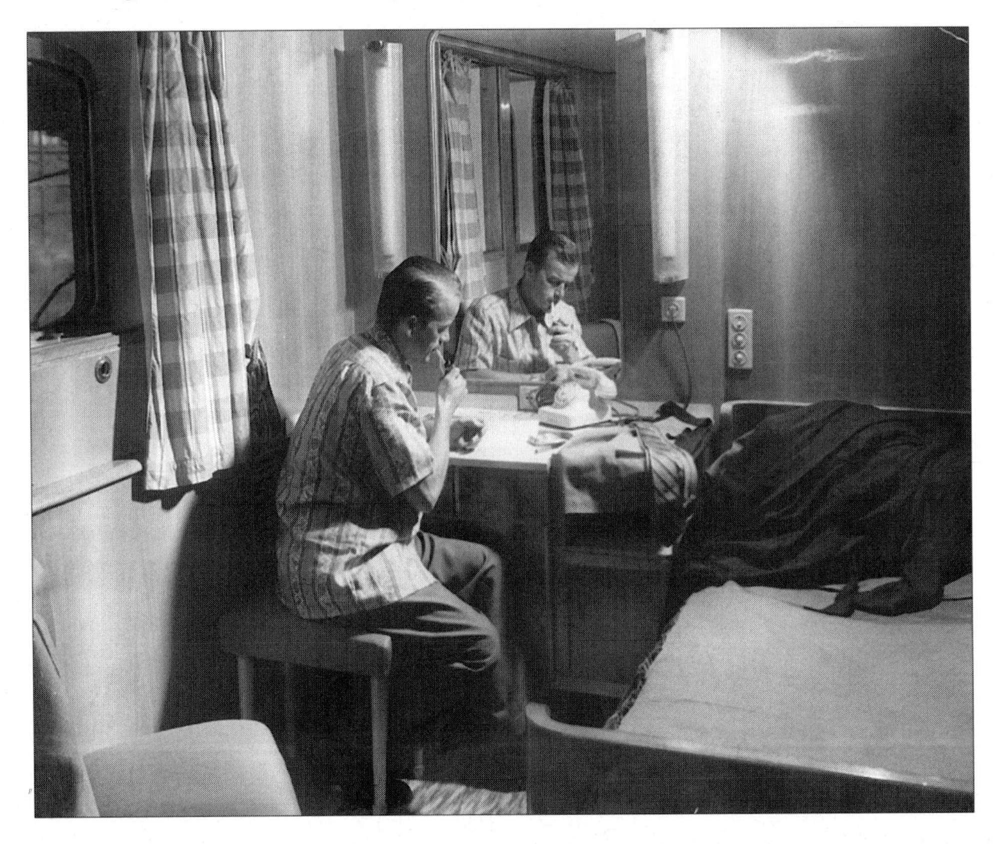

ANDREA DORIA
ANDREA DORIA
GENOVA

Not everyone was fond of the then-current design trends. "I am not a fan of '50s ocean liner decor and so it is difficult for me to be complimentary," stated Frank Trumbour. "I will say, however, that as time has passed, I am more tolerant of the interior decoration of that period, but I think this feeling is more of nostalgia than an appreciation for the decor itself. Perhaps the *Doria,* as well as the *Colombo,* suffered the same fate as other liners of that era—they left you feeling somewhat cold. Certainly, they were far more inviting than the beloved, but sterile, *United States*. But I do not think that the Italian liners of that period were inviting. It was their exteriors that was inviting." While not as lavish as those in first class, here we see three tourist-class public rooms: the bar-lounge, ***opposite, top,*** the card room, ***opposite, bottom,*** and the writing room–library, ***above.***

Tourist class offered economical travel for tourists, students and westbound immigrants. This view shows an inside four-berth cabin, ***below.*** A berth in peak summer season was priced at $250 per person for the eight-day voyage from New York to Naples.

At the end of each crossing, the *Andrea Doria,* like other Italian liners, would reach the outer part of New York harbor in the predawn hours. Usually, they would pass through the Narrows and along the Lower Bay by six o'clock, and then be safely and securely docked at Pier 84 by eight o'clock. In this instance, however, the *Doria* is making a midday arrival. Sharing Pier 84 with the American Export Lines (with frequent visits of their *Independence* and *Constitution*), often left only one berth for the Italian Line. Consequently, as seen in this 1955 photo from the outbound *Vulcania,* ***above,*** the older ship departed at noon and thereby freed the berth. The *Doria* has delayed her arrival and, occupying that same berth at Pier 84, will tie-up at one in the afternoon, as seen here with a Moran tug assisting, ***opposite.***

ANDREA DORIA

In a panoramic view from the top of the Empire State Building, we see the portion of the Hudson River and great piers known as "Luxury Liner Row." Using Pier 84, seen in the center of this photo with the *Andrea Doria* at berth, ***above,*** the Italian liners tended to stay one or two nights. There would be off-loading of the inbound passengers and cargo, some onboard cleaning and light repairs, refueling, and then taking on the outbound passengers and cargo. In this Saturday afternoon view, the piers are quite empty except for two other liners, Cunard's *Britannic* and the Furness-Bermuda Line's *Ocean Monarch* to the right. Across the river are the waterfront communities of Weehawken and Edgewater, both in New Jersey. In the distance are the famed New Jersey Meadowlands.

"While the Italian Line ships were very popular in the postwar years, in the 1950s and '60s, I do not believe that they received quite the same grand attention that the Cunarders and the French Line ships did, even though they were great treasures in their own right," noted Frank Trumbour. "In the prewar years, they had all the glamor and style one could want, as in a Hollywood movie. In postwar, they represented the renaissance of a great tradition. They had the appeal of the Mediterranean, marvelous food, and the warmth of Italian crews. They added a wonderful dimension to the sea-going transportation network of the world." The romance of the great liners was quite stirring at night when the ships, their funnels and decks were illuminated. In this poetic view taken from the foot of West 46th Street, ***opposite, top,*** we see the *Andrea Doria* to the left, and the *America* of United States Lines to the right.

Because of her short, three-year career, the *Andrea Doria* did not appear in many of the great gatherings of ocean liners along Manhattan's West Side. On this rare occasion on July 4, 1956, which proved, in fact, to be her last call at New York, she is gathered with no less than six other liners, ***opposite, bottom.*** From left to right, there is the *Media, Caronia,* and *Queen Mary* of Cunard Line; the *Liberté,* French Line; the *United States* and *America,* United States Lines; and finally the *Doria.*

EVANS
AMERICA

UNITED STATES LINES
AMERICAN EXPORT LINES

While in port, at Pier 84, the Italian liners were often used for luncheons, dinners, commemorative occasions, and tours by travel agents. In this view, ***top,*** we see New York City's top restauranteurs being hosted at a luncheon sponsored by Martini & Rossi.

Celebrities from all walks of life were often photographed on the decks of the *Andrea Doria* and other Italian liners usually as they sailed for Europe. In these photos, we see Anna Magnani and Tennessee Williams, ***middle,*** Francis Cardinal Spellman, ***bottom,*** Kim Novak, ***opposite, top,*** Gracie Fields, ***opposite, middle,*** and Christine Jorgensen, ***opposite, bottom.***

Most often, the *Andrea Doria* would depart from Pier 84 at noon. Within thirty minutes, she would be moving down the Hudson and passing Lower Manhattan. From the stern, ***opposite, top,*** we can see two shuttling Erie Railroad ferries, the Empire State Building (to the right), and, in the distance on the left, the upper Hudson. From the top deck, ***opposite, bottom,*** we see the famed New York City skyline with the Woolworth Building on the left.

"From the sleek funnels to the delicate curves of practically every hull plate to the flare of the bows, the Italian genius at making the functional very beautiful achieved sublime perfection with the exteriors of the turbo nave *Andrea Doria* and her sister, the *Cristoforo Colombo,*" said Sal Scannella.

In this romantic view, ***above,*** the *Doria*'s great funnel and a portion of her upper decks share the setting with the Lower Manhattan skyline. Soon, the great liner will pass out of the harbor and put to sea. A journey begins. The Italian Line said of the beginning of a voyage, "In a few short hours all sight of land disappears . . . and a new adventure begins! Cares of the workaday world slip away as though they never existed . . . for you are in a world apart. And you'll enjoy this new world to its fullest from the wide decks of the *Andrea Doria*. From the Belvedere Deck, you'll watch the fascinating play of light and shadow on the restless waves. From the glass-sheltered Promenade Deck, you'll enjoy the ever-changing colors of a clear sunset. From the curving stern decks, you'll watch the disappearing wake of a ship that plies the Sunny Southern Route."

Clear skies with warm sunshine gave way to a foggy night on July 25, 1956, the day before the *Andrea Doria* was due in New York. She was on a regular westbound crossing, steaming at 21 knots on her usual routing from Naples, Genoa, Cannes, and Gibraltar. Among the 1,708 passengers and crew aboard, the first-class passenger list included Hollywood actress Ruth Roman, several American politicians, a pair of European ballet dancers, and the mayor of Philadelphia. With the evening fog, her captain began to worry that he might have to reduce speed and therefore delay her arrival at Pier 84, closely scheduled by the home office for eight the next morning. At eleven o'clock that morning, the Swedish American liner *Stockholm* had left Pier 97—thirteen New York City blocks north of the Italian Line terminal—on an eastbound crossing to Copenhagen and Gothenburg. Thirty minutes later, from Pier 88, at West 48th Street, French Line's *Ile de France* cast off, also on an eastward passage, to Plymouth and Le Havre. All three ships would, quite unexpectedly, have a fateful meeting later that night.

At eleven o'clock that night, in thickening fog off Nantucket, the officers aboard the *Doria* noticed the lights of another ship. Radar had not yet been perfected, and the first pip of that other ship was miscalculated and quickly came much closer. She was believed to be a small freighter. In fact, it was the *Stockholm*. The two liners were traveling at a combined speed of 40 knots (or 46 miles per hour) and therefore moving at the rate of approximately one mile per minute. At 11:21 P.M., the *Stockholm* materialized out of the fog and rammed into the *Doria*. The stricken ship abruptly and dramatically lurched over to port and then righted. Passengers and crew heard the sounds of a grinding crash, and some saw the bright lights of the *Stockholm* through the *Doria*'s windows and portholes. The Swedish ship's reinforced bow was like a dagger piercing the larger Italian. She cut forty feet into the *Doria*'s hull, just below the bridge, creating a jagged hole like an inverted pyramid that extended from below the waterline up to B Deck. It was a mortal wound. The two liners were entangled together for a short time until movement tore them apart. Fifty-five feet of the *Stockholm*'s foredeck and bow were folded into a tangled mass of steel. The *Doria* sent out an immediate SOS and began the starboard list from which she would never recover, ***above.*** With her fuel tanks empty, she had very little ballast. The ships were some 45 miles south of Nantucket Island, a sea-lane known as the "Crossroads of the Atlantic" because of its busy shipping pattern. No less than eleven U.S. Coast Guard cutters were immediately dispatched to sea following the first calls for help from the stricken *Doria*. "The *Andrea Doria* could also have caught fire with the great impact of the collision with the *Stockholm,*" observed Captain Ed Squire, "but fortunately this was not an added problem in that tragedy."

It was soon realized that the badly damaged *Stockholm* was in no danger of sinking, and so she began to assist the doomed *Doria*. Below decks on the Italian ship, crewmen struggled quickly and furiously to pump out the floods of invading Atlantic water. Deck crews worked promptly to rig rope ladders and nets so passengers could clamber down the ship's sides and reach waiting lifeboats. All the port-side lifeboats were useless because of the severe, ever-increasing list to starboard. The *Doria*'s electrical system fortunately continued to work, along with the huge boat deck emergency searchlights. The caption for this photo, ***below,*** taken at about two-thirty in the morning by Ken Gouldthorpe, a passenger aboard the assisting *Ile de France*, read, "Lighted up, and with searchlights acting as beacons for lifeboats, the stricken *Andrea Doria* lists badly."

Passengers slid down ropes—off the stern, off the bow, off the quarter. Small children and the elderly were carried. The steady relay of lifeboats, while largely successful, was frequently a clumsy affair throughout the night. The boats, often unwieldy, were manned by cooks, waiters, and bellhops. The *Doria*'s whistle moaned continuously—her death rattle. A small armada of ships began to gather around the liner as passengers and crew fled for safety. For a time, radio traffic between the rescue ships, as well as shore, became overloaded and confusing. By daylight, the *Doria* was keeled well over and all but abandoned, ***above.*** The last of the passengers were removed by five o'clock in the morning, over five hours following the collision. Only Captain Calamai and a few officers remained aboard, hoping that the stricken liner might somehow be saved. Below, the pumps still throbbed as tons of seawater was pumped overboard—to no avail.

Seen here from the waiting *Ile de France* and with the transport *Sgt. Joseph E. Kelly* off to the right, the cutter *Hornbeam* eased alongside the Italian flagship at six in the morning, ***above.*** There was no hope. The captain and his last remaining crewmembers were taken off the sinking liner. Frank Trumbour recalled hearing the first reports of the sinking. "I was nine years old at the time and we were returning late in the evening from a trip to the New Jersey shore," he recalled. "The car radio was on and the news flash came over that the *Andrea Doria* was sinking. Everyone in the car was shocked at the news. Naturally, the next day, we watched the television reports and followed the events as they unfolded. It all made a very dramatic impression on a boy of nine."

"I was working in Lower Manhattan, in the shipping district in Bowling Green, at the time of the *Doria*'s collision and sinking. It was the morning of the 26th," added Richard Faber. "It was a total shock. Not since the *Titanic,* forty-four years before, had anything like this happened with a big Atlantic ocean liner."

"Both Moran Towing and the salvage company, Merritt, Chapman & Scott, were called by the Italian Line as the *Doria* was sinking. They discussed towing the stricken liner and beaching her, possibly on the shores of Nantucket," recalled Captain Ed Squire. "But there was not enough time. She was sinking far too quickly. Furthermore, with the great list, ***opposite, top,*** she might well have turned over completely if a tow was attempted. Realistically, she could not have withstood the stress of a towline."

While the damaged *Stockholm* waits off to the left in this photograph, ***opposite, bottom,*** the epic drama was nearing a dramatic, very tragic end by nine o'clock in the morning. It was three hours since Captain Calamai had bid her farewell. Silent passengers, crew, and other seafarers watched transfixed as the abandoned *Andrea Doria,* with her huge funnel, the outer decks, and three swimming pools clearly visible, begins her final hour.

"I was at the end of a one-year fellowship as an architectural apprentice in the summer of 1956," recalled Der Scutt. "I decided to travel for two months before returning to the United States. I wanted to visit the south of France and Italy, and had a reservation on the *Andrea Doria* for my trip home. I would have reached New York on July 26, 1956. But after I arrived early in Geneva, I decided I could see more of Belgium and the Netherlands, and visit London by taking three extra weeks. Fortunately, while in London, I was able to change reservations to the *Mauretania,* which was sailing from Southampton. I was stunned when I heard about the tragedy, the sinking of the *Doria,* which I would have been part of had I not changed my plans. I would have lost a year's work of special drawings. All my photos, diaries, and books would have perished!"

In chronicling the worst ocean liner disaster of its time, journalist Edward F. Oliver wrote, "The *Andrea Doria* rolled bottom up, thrust her glistening propellers into the sunlight and then plunged to the ocean's floor. Her voyage had ended." The U.S. Coast Guard cutter *Evergreen* flashed the official obituary to the world: "SS *Andrea Doria* sank in 225 feet of water at 10:09 A.M." The cutter marked the grave with a floating tombstone—a yellow buoy. 1,662 were saved, fifty-two were lost—forty-six from the *Doria* and six from the *Stockholm*. Now, the ships that had kept the deathwatch got underway, ***above.***

"The sinking of the *Andrea Doria* holds special memories for many ocean liner buffs and historians," concluded Scutt. "Her tragedy was like losing one of your beloved children. It had contributed so much love and now it was gone! The Italians strove for unrivaled authority, fantasy, and symbolism, especially with the *Doria*."

Extensive, very confidential inquiries and hearings followed the tragedy. Final compensation amounted to $48 million, but no precise responsibility was determined. The final investigation and findings were dropped by the mutual consent of both the Italian Line and the Swedish American Line. The disaster did lead, however, to greatly increased radar navigation training for ships' officers.

By 2004, forty-eight years after her sinking, the wreckage of the *Andrea Doria* was deteriorating at an increasing speed, possibly due to the global warming of the seawater. Her funnel and upper decks are gone, disintegrated down to the promenade deck area. Over forty divers have been lost in their attempts to reach the sunken liner. A lure to countless divers, remnants from the ship—from restaurant china to medicine bottles from the ship's hospital—have been retrieved. Even the statue of Andrea Doria has been removed. A lifeboat washed ashore on Staten Island twenty-six years later, in 1982. The *Doria* also remains very popular in the ocean liner collectibles market. A photo postcard, for example, currently sells for $25, while a fold-out deck plan is tagged at approximately $125. A bound book of interior photographs goes for $5,000, while a ceramic tile from the ship's first-class bar changed hands for $6,000. A weathered life jacket sold recently on the auction market for several thousand dollars.

Plans to salvage the *Doria* made news for some years after the sinking. There were reports that huge chains would be affixed to the hull and then it would be dragged near shore and raised. Another was to fill the hull with huge numbers of ping-pong balls and therein refloat it. Nothing came to pass, of course, and in the end the Italian Line abandoned the wreckage to the underwriters. Following the abandonment of the final investigations, the *Andrea Doria* was never again mentioned by the Italian Line.

STOCKHOLM. Sad and almost disgraced, indeed the villain to many, the badly damaged *Stockholm* dragged itself back to Pier 97 in New York, ***opposite, top,*** where her voyage had begun. She was actually the last of a virtual caravan of rescue ships that arrived in New York harbor: the *Ile de France* was first, with 758 survivors; the *Cape Ann,* with 129; the *Pvt. William H. Thomas,* 158; and the *Edward H. Allen,* 76. The wounded but gallant *Stockholm* delivered 533 survivors. She crept through the water at reduced speed to protect her forward bulkhead. On either side, ready for any further emergency, the Coast Guard cutters *Tamaroa* and *Owasco,* along with the government tug *Mahoning,* kept her company. Newsmen and photographers aboard tugs and hired craft met these ships, especially the *Stockholm,* at the outer reaches of New York harbor. Never had the little Swede been photographed so often. She moved slowly and cautiously, into the Upper Bay and then along the Hudson. Anxious reporters yelled questions to crewmen, survivors, the *Stockholm*'s passengers, to anyone who might respond. This was the biggest news story of the day and everyone looked for a reason, someone to blame, for the tragic collision. [Built by A/B Gotaverken Shipyard, Gothenburg, Sweden, 1948. 12,644 gross tons; 525 feet long; 69 feet wide. Gotaverken diesels, twin screw. Service speed 19 knots. 608 passengers in 1955 (24 first-class, 584 tourist-class).]

***Opposite, bottom*:** The sight of the *Stockholm*'s bow—now smashed, mangled, and twisted—brought home the true impact of the enormous, penetrating collision between two ocean liners. It seemed as if the Swedish ship was beyond repair. How could the bow—which had been specially strengthened against the ice of the North Atlantic—be repaired and rebuilt?

CKHOLM.
TEBORG

CKHOLM

Swedish American Line had the good fortune to have their ship repaired within the confines of New York harbor. Bethlehem Steel Company representatives and engineers went immediately to Pier 97 after the ship's arrival. They were confident that they could repair her and, rather quickly, the task was assigned and the ship moved to the lower Brooklyn waterfront, to Bethlehem's plant at 56th Street. There, in a floating dry dock normally used by the likes of the far bigger *Independence* and *Constitution,* the *Stockholm* took her place for over four months, ***above.*** The wreckage was cleared and the bow section was completely rebuilt, allowing for the ship's return to Sweden that December.

The *Stockholm* continued in Swedish American Line's transatlantic service for another three years, until December 1959. Then, no longer suited to the demands of that service because of her small size and passenger-cargo configuration, she was sold to the East German government and became the world's first Communist Party trade union cruise ship, the *Volkerfreundschaft* ("International Friendship"). She traveled mostly to either Soviet or other Communist ports, including Havana. Exhausted and withdrawn in 1985, she did a stint at Oslo as the refugee accommodation ship *Fridtjok Nansen* before, in an unexpected turn of fate, she was sold to Italian buyers in 1989.

ILE DE FRANCE. The legendary *Ile de France,* steaming eastbound to Europe, was forty miles from the collision scene. Hearing the distress calls, she had reversed course and sped to the site, with her two red and black funnels aglow, and her name in red neon letters spelled out along the top decks. Taking on an impressive 758 survivors, her master was seen as a modern-day hero while the press highlighted the great French liner's gallant role in the tragedy. She is seen here in New York's Lower Bay, ***opposite, top,*** her decks crowded with passengers, crew, and survivors alike. Later, the *Ile de France* was presented with a Gallant Ship Award by the U.S. Coast Guard, where it remains with the French Line archives at Le Havre to this day.

The *Ile de France* did only another two years of Atlantic service when, due to old age, she was retired. Sold to Japanese shipbreakers in December 1958, she had something of reprieve when she was used as a floating prop in the disaster film *The Last Voyage,* starring Robert Stack and Dorothy Malone, before being broken-up at Osaka. [Built by Chantiers de l'Atlantique, St Nazaire, France, 1927. 44,356 gross tons; 792 feet long; 91 feet wide. Steam turbines, quadruple screw. Service speed 23½ knots. 1,345 passengers after 1949 (541 first-class, 577 cabin-class, 227 tourist-class).]

CAPE ANN. Fifteen miles to the northeast, the freighter *Cape Ann* found herself nearest to the collision scene. Nearby was the U.S. military troop transport *Pvt. William H. Thomas,* the destroyer USS *Edward H. Allen* (out on gunnery practice), the American tanker *Robert E. Hopkins,* the Danish freighter *Laura Maersk,* the banana boat *Manaqu,* the British freighters *Tyrone* and *Tarantia,* and another American troop transport, the *Sgt. Joseph E. Kelly.* The *Cape Ann,* ***opposite, bottom,*** was one of United Fruit Company's break-bulk freighters, not one of their traditional "banana boats." In July 1956, she was not sailing in the tropical trades, but on the North Atlantic, making a charter voyage from Bremerhaven to New York for another American shipowner, the Isbrandtsen Line. This brought her to a fateful position in the *Andrea Doria* tragedy.

The *Cape Ann* had been built as a wartime transport and then was sold to the United Fruit Company in 1947. She and several identical sisters that sailed mostly from eastern U.S. ports to the Caribbean, as well as Central and South American ports. She was sold in 1963 to American Union Transport and renamed *Transunion.* Her end came in 1968, when she was broken-up on Taiwan. [Built by Consolidated Steel Corporation, Wilmington, California, 1943. 6,750 gross tons; 417 feet long; 60 feet wide. Steam turbines, single screw. Service speed 14 knots. 12 passengers.]

CONTE GRANDE. In September 1956, some six weeks after the sinking of the *Andrea Doria,* Italian Line hurriedly moved the *Conte Grande,* ***above,*** off the Italy–South America route for a roundtrip voyage to New York. She helped to handle the overflow of otherwise-stranded passengers left by the loss of the *Doria.* In a further reshuffling, the *Augustus* would be moved off the South American run as well, beginning in February 1957, for nine months of sailings on the express run to and from New York.

LAST OF THE SURVIVORS. Of all the ships involved in the *Andrea Doria* sinking, only the former *Stockholm* lives on at the time of writing. She turned fifty-six in 2004. She had not been expected to have so long a life. In a strange twist of fate, she sailed into Genoa in 1989 and became an Italian cruise ship in the early 1990s. Gutted and thoroughly rebuilt as a very modern passenger ship carrying 566 all-first-class passengers, she sailed first as the *Italia Prima* for her Naples-based owners, Nina Cruise Lines. Beginning in 1998, on charter to another Italian firm, the Valtur Corporation, she sailed on Caribbean cruises that including stopovers in Cuba as the *Valtur Prima,* seen here arriving in Havana, ***below.*** In 2002, she continued in this Caribbean service, but as the *Caribe,* on charter to a Greek line, Festival Cruises. When Festival collapsed into bankruptcy in early 2004, the liner was sold that August to Lisbon-based Classic Cruises International. She is now the *Athena,* sailing on Mediterranean and South American itineraries.

CHAPTER FIVE

A Glorious Twin Sister: The *Cristoforo Colombo*

Lewis and Ruth Gordon made over one hundred crossings of the great North Atlantic, beginning with a honeymoon trip from New York to Southampton on the *Queen Mary* in July 1937. For some thirty years, from 1947 until the mid-1970s, they crossed annually, going in both directions by liner. They sailed with all the great companies such as Cunard, French Line, American Export, and Holland America, but the couple especially enjoyed the Italian Line. They loved its renowned service, food, and shipboard atmosphere. In the course of their summertime excursions, they sampled almost all of the great Italian Line passenger ships.

Early trips were aboard the likes of the *Vulcania* and *Conte Biancamano*. But Italian Line began adding new liners, each of them fast, modern, and more comfortable, in the 1950s. There were the sisters *Augustus* and *Giulio Cesare* (1951–52), then the *Andrea Doria* and *Cristoforo Colombo* (1953–54), and then the *Leonardo da Vinci* (1960). "We came home on the *Augustus* and the *Giulio Cesare,*" noted Mr. Gordon. "They were very modern ships, very different from the old *Vulcania*. Typically, there were lots of families with children on those late August sailings from Naples, Genoa, Cannes, and Gibraltar to New York. There was great competition with the American Export Lines and their twin sister ships, the *Independence* and *Constitution*. Those American ships were very modern, with all sorts of novel features, but Italian Line had superior food and very gracious waiters. The Italians were also very generous with their portions and even suggested filet mignon for breakfast!"

The Gordons also sailed from New York to Casablanca on the *Andrea Doria* and later crossed back on her sister, the *Cristoforo Colombo*. "I recall the *Doria,* then almost brand-new, as being a very beautiful ship. Altogether, there were four or five outdoor pools. One or two were shallow and just for children. The decor was the most modern yet on the Italian Line, and the entertainment included horse racing and a dance team. On the *Colombo,* we stopped at Boston on the day after sailing from New York and we were able to have my son come aboard for lunch. He was then at MIT as a student and this was an added bonus! I also recall the boys in small boats that surrounded us at anchor off Gibraltar. They swam, dove, and did tricks for coins. They also displayed handicrafts from their open boats. The passengers on deck would send money wrapped in paper, which was placed in wicker baskets that were lifted and lowered with string. The purchases were then hoisted aboard."

Prior to the flood of publicity following the *Andrea Doria's* tragic sinking, the Italian Line paid slightly more attention in their mid-1950s advertising, news releases, and promotional literature, to the *Cristoforo Colombo*. She was the newer, slightly larger, and, for some, more luxuriously appointed of the pair. Here, in a scene dating from March 1954, we see her massive funnel lying in the Ansaldo shipyard prior to being lifted aboard, ***opposite, top.*** Her maiden crossing to New York came four months later, in July. [Built by Ansaldo Shipyards, Genoa, Italy, 1954. 29,191 gross tons; 700 feet long; 90 feet wide. Steam turbines, twin screw. Service speed 23 knots. 1,055 passengers (229 first-class, 222 cabin-class, 604 tourist-class).]

In this 1958 photograph at Genoa, the *Cristoforo Colombo's* superb good looks are very evident, ***opposite, bottom.*** She was one of the most beautiful of all Atlantic liners of that period. And as a consequence of the *Doria's* sinking, she reigned as the flagship of the Italian merchant marine, as well as of the Italian Line itself, from the summer of 1956 until the arrival of the new *Leonardo da Vinci* in the summer of 1960. Two other liners, the French *Provence* and the *Giulio Cesare,* are to the right of the *Colombo.*

Here we see several examples of the decor onboard the *Cristoforo Colombo:* the first-class verandah, ***above,*** and the first-class smoking room and bar, ***below.***

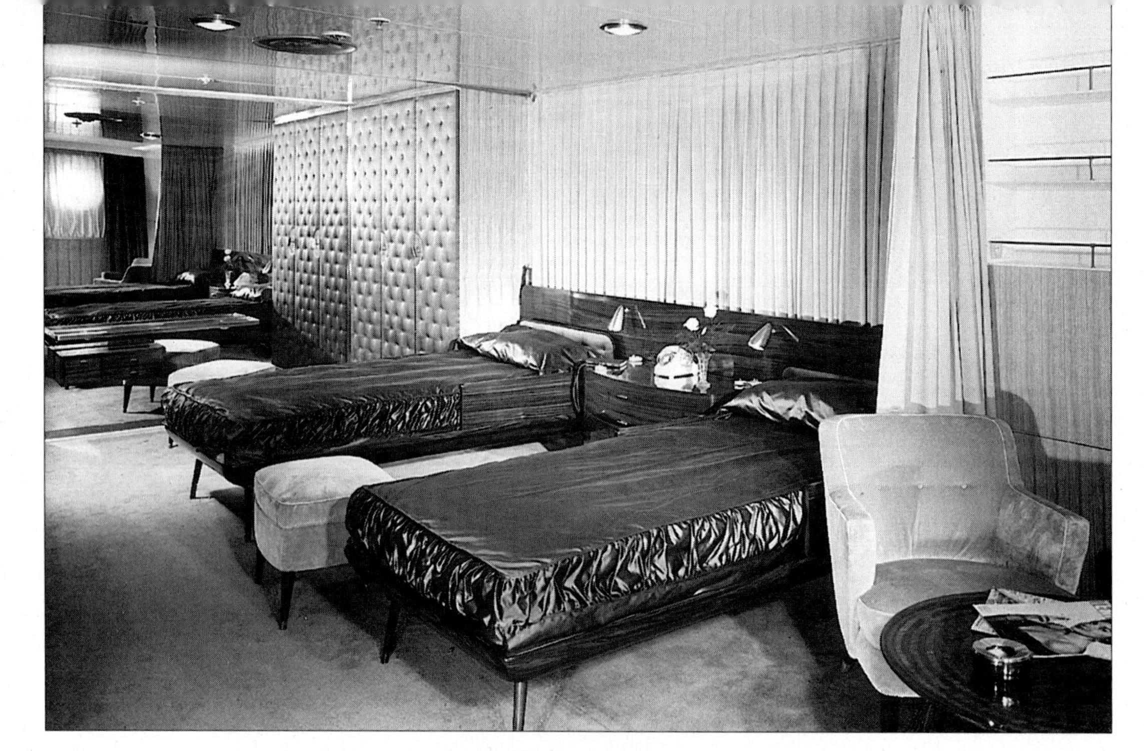

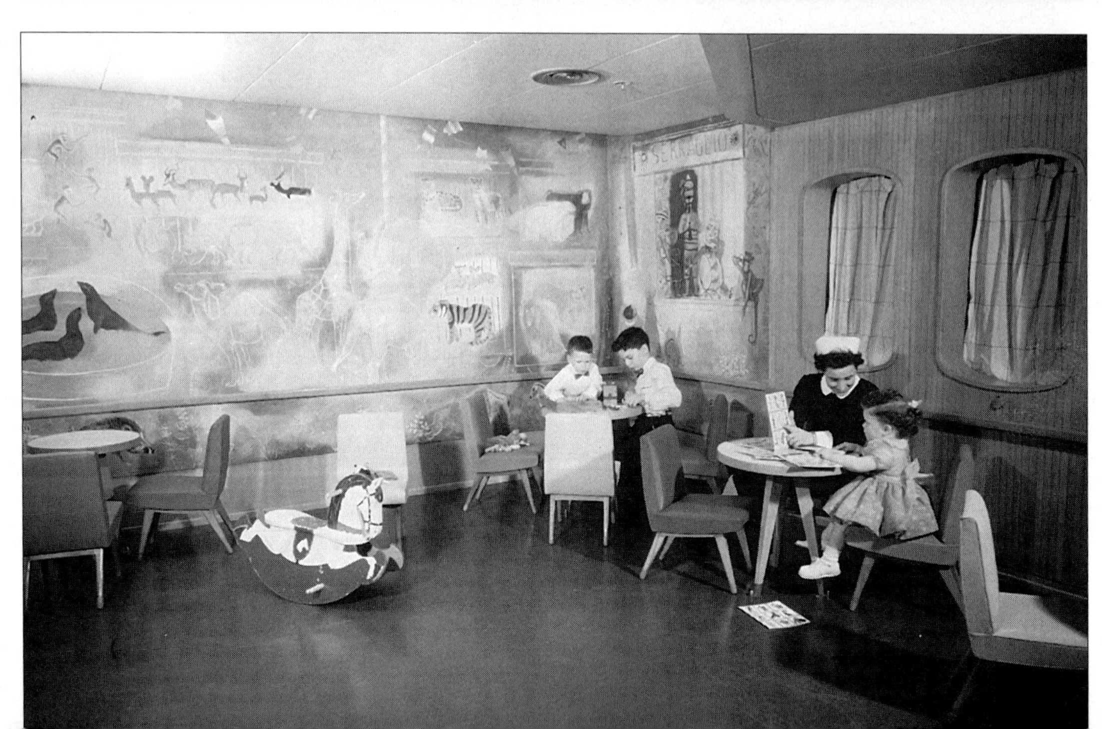

Shown here are several examples of living quarters aboard the *Cristoforo Colombo,* including a first-class suite, ***opposite, top,*** a first-class double, ***opposite, middle,*** and the children's playroom, ***opposite, bottom.*** Like the *Doria,* she was one of the most modern liners plying the Atlantic in the 1950s. "The interiors of the *Doria* and *Colombo* were glamorous statements of '50s design," said Charles Howland. "They were ultra-modern in age that worshiped the 'new.' As a modernist, I appreciate the forward-looking optimism their interiors represented. Those interiors were miles ahead of the French, British, and American ships of the era."

The *Cristoforo Colombo* remained on Naples–Genoa–New York express run until the spring of 1965, with the debut of the brand-new superliners *Michelangelo* and *Raffaello.* She was then moved onto the more extensive Adriatic service, sailing out of Trieste and Venice and calling at the likes of Dubrovnik, Patras or Piraeus, Messina, Palermo, Barcelona, and Lisbon. Single-handedly, she replaced the veteran team of *Saturnia* and *Vulcania.* The Adriatic service to New York was dropped in the face of greatly increased airline competition, however, by the winter of 1973, and the *Colombo* was used to replace the mechanically troubled *Giulio Cesare* on the eastern South American coast route. Now sailing to the likes of Rio, Santos, Montevideo, and Buenos Aires, she was paired with the *Augustus* and later with the *Guglielmo Marconi,* which was on loan from Lloyd Triestino's fast-fading Australian trade. Historically, the *Colombo* closed down Italian Line's South American passenger service in the spring of 1977. She is seen here, ***above,*** making her final departure from Santos, in a lovely scene dated April 5, 1977.

In the mid-1970s, the Italian Line was busily selling off its passenger ship fleet. While the *Giulio Cesare* had gone to the breakers in 1973, the ten-year-old, money-losing sisters *Michelangelo* and *Raffaello* were decommissioned in 1975 and sold two years later to the Iranian government. The *Augustus* was finished in 1976, as were the "Three Musicians"—the *Donizetti, Rossini,* and *Verdi.* The *Colombo* ended her Italian sailing days in 1977, and the struggling *Leonardo da Vinci* a year later. In those fuel-expensive times in the mid-1970s, the *Colombo,* while still a useful ship at twenty-three, could not find a buyer interested in sailing her. Instead, she was sold to Venezuelans, who used her as a moored accommodation ship for workers at Puerto Ordaz. When that task ended in 1981, again there were no buyers, and so she was sold to the hungry scrap-metal merchants of Taiwan. Rusted and forlorn, the former Italian Line flagship and sister ship to the legendary *Andrea Doria* was towed slowly across the Pacific for demolition at Kaohsiung. Once there, however, the Taiwanese had new, albeit short-lived ideas that perhaps she could find a buyer and had her moved to Hong Kong. As shown here, ***above,*** she was anchored in Hong Kong harbor for several months, awaiting inspection teams and possible new owners. But nothing came to pass and, in the fall of 1982, the liner was towed back to Kaohsiung and finished off. The year before, the burnt-out corpse of the *Leonardo da Vinci* was broken-up; just months later, in February 1983, the *Raffaello* was bombed and sunk in an Iraqi air raid on the Iranian port of Bushire. From then on, only the former *Augustus* and *Michelangelo* remained afloat, but in far-off shores and under different owners.

CHAPTER SIX

Fleetmates: Other Italian Passenger Ships

In the first edition of Laurence Dunn's splendid *Passenger Liners,* the definitive directory of world passenger ships first published in 1961, the section on Italian passenger ships was the second largest in the book. Only the British had more passenger vessels at the time. It had only been five years since the *Andrea Doria* had perished, and Italy was in its peak, post-war passenger ship period. Business to almost all parts of the world and in all classes—from luxurious first class to the sometimes-austere tourist and third—was booming. And through the Italian Line offices in the United States, passengers could book aboard one of the company's ships and connect to each of the four corners of the earth from the likes of Genoa, Naples, Venice, or Trieste. A rack in the Italian Line's Lower Manhattan offices offered a range of materials—brochures, sailing schedules, rate sheets, and the like—to the interested public.

The Italian government's Finmare Group controlled the nation's four largest passenger ship fleets: the Italian Line, which connected Europe with both North and South America; Lloyd Triestino, which offered links to south and east Africa, as well Middle and Far Eastern ports; Adriatica Line, which connected Italy with the Eastern Mediterranean, including Egypt, Israel, Lebanon, and Syria; and the Tirrenia Lines, which offered local services in and around Italy. Altogether, the four companies had over four-dozen passenger ships, headed by Italian Line's splendid new 33,000-ton *Leonardo da Vinci.* And four very fast and large liners were in the works by 1961—the 45,000-ton sisters *Michelangelo* and *Raffaello* for the Italian Line, and the 27,000-ton pair *Guglielmo Marconi* and *Galileo Galilei* for Lloyd Triestino.

Italy had also been well known, especially after World War II, for having national shipowners that specialized in converting older, secondhand passenger ships, freighters, and even small aircraft carriers for low-fare, tourist, and immigrant services. By the 1960s, trade to South America and especially Australia, both of which offered promising new opportunities, was virtually overflowing. There was the Cogedar Line, which ran two converted passenger ships in 1961 (the *Aurelia* and the *Flaminia),* and was expanding with their largest ship to date—the lavish conversion of Cunard's 250-passenger *Media* into the 1,320-berth *Flavia.* The Grimaldi-Siosa Lines ran three veteran liners, each of which was periodically modernized and improved, in the Central American trades. They were the *Venezuela* (1924), the *Florida* (1926), and the *Irpinia* (1929). Flotta Lauro of Naples ran two rebuilt World War II "baby flattops," the *Roma* (1946) and the *Sydney* (1944), as well as a vintage, former American passenger ship, the *Surriento,* which had been the Grace Line's *Santa Maria* of 1928. Lauro was, in 1961, also thinking of building their first new liners (27,000 tons each, as first planned) for the still very brisk Australian market. By 1964, however, it decided in favor of further secondhand, rebuilt tonnage: the former Dutch liners *Oranje* and *Willem Ruys,* which were dramatically transformed into the very modern *Angelina Lauro* and *Achille Lauro.* The Sitmar Line also had three greatly rebuilt veteran ships, all used on the Europe-Australia route, as well as around-the-world tourist services. The *Fairsea* and *Fairsky,* both built in 1941, were former aircraft carriers that were evidently well-suited for rebuilding with no less than just short of 1,500 passenger berths each. Sitmar's third ship, the *Castel Felice,* which also had an enlarged capacity of over 1,400, had been the *Kenya,* a British India Line passenger-cargo ship completed in 1930. Finally, Genoa-headquartered Costa Line was perhaps the fastest growing of the companies interested largely in rebuilding older ships in the early 1960s. While it had commissioned their first new build in 1958, the superb *Federico C,* for the busy South American east coast run, the company also had such ships as the rebuilt *Bianca C* (1949), *Anna C* (1929), *Andrea C* (1942), and, by far the eldest of all the Italian-flag passenger ships of the period, the *Franca C* (1914). Like Italian Line, Lloyd Triestino, and Lauro, the Costa Line was also looking to expand and add further liner tonnage. It opted for a newbuild and produced the magnificent, 30,000-ton *Eugenio C,* completed in 1966.

The Home Lines was, like Sitmar, not completely Italian, but multinational. It was generally thought of as Italian, at least in Laurence Dunn's book, because of its largely Italian officers and crew, cuisine, style of service, and management through the port of Genoa. Primarily interested in the more demanding American trades, both on the Atlantic and for alternative, wintertime cruises, Home Lines lovingly restored and refitted their three liners in service in 1961: the *Homeric* (the former *Mariposa)* of 1931, the *Italia* (the former *Kungsholm)* of 1928, and the *Queen Frederica* (the former *Malolo)* of 1927. The latter ship was actually operated by a Home Lines' subsidiary, the Athens-based National Hellenic American Line, and even flew the Greek flag, but was considered a member of the Home Lines family. Home Lines was also making major plans at the time for a 39,000-tonner for continued Europe–Eastern Canada service. But while under construction, the futuristic, innovative *Oceanic,* was reassigned to what was fast becoming a far more promising part of the ocean liner business: year-round, all-one-class cruising. That 1,200-berth ship was indeed a great sign of the future.

This entire network of passenger ship services was, of course, gradually and then quite dramatically changing. Lloyd Triestino's *Marconi* and *Galileo* of 1963 were, in fact, the last newly built Italians for the Australian run while Costa's *Eugenio C,* commissioned three years later, was the final Italian liner built for the South American trade. The traditional, class-divided, port-to-port passenger ship business was declining in the face of increasing airline competition. By the 1970s, most of these companies turned to more profitable cruise service. While the likes of Cogedar, Home Lines, Italian Line, Lauro, Lloyd Triestino, and Sitmar are now gone, others reinvented themselves for the expanding Italian and international cruise markets. Costa, for example, now part of the huge, Miami-based Carnival Cruise Lines empire, has eleven passenger ships, Costa's largest liner fleet ever. Grimaldi lives on as well and operates mega-ferry cruise ships. A new addition, Mediterranean Shipping Cruises, appeared in the Italian passenger ship business in the 1990s, with recent expansions that include an order of two 85,000-ton cruise ship in late 2003, and the purchase of twin 58,000-tonners in 2004.

The great and vast Italian passenger ship fleet of the early 1960s has changed almost beyond recognition, but remains today in the current guise of cruising, with those lavish, white-hulled, lido-deck-lined floating resorts. The fleet is certainly bigger and perhaps even better than ever.

OCEANIA. To replace heavy war losses, Trieste-based Lloyd Triestino ordered no less than seven new passenger-cargo liners in the late 1940s. Lloyd Triestino, which, like the Italian Line, was part of the government-controlled Finmare Group, was formed in 1837 and was said to be the oldest shipping company still in business by the 1960s. The company's interests lay in the African, Asian, and Pacific trades. For the run to Australia from Italy, the first three new-builds were the *Australia, Neptunia,* and *Oceania* (seen here arriving at Melbourne for the first time on September 13, 1951, ***above***). Like Italian Line's *Giulio Cesare* and *Augustus,* these Lloyd Triestino sisters were very significant to Italy, and the Italian marine and shipbuilding industries—they signaled a rebirth following the devastation of World War II. The *Oceania* and her two sisters were routed from Genoa, Naples, and Messina to Port Said, Suez, Aden, Colombo, Djakarta, Fremantle, Melbourne, and Sydney. Their quarters ranged from twin-bedded suites in first class to twenty-two-berth dormitories in tourist class. [Built by Cantieri Riuniti dell'Adriatico, Trieste, Italy, 1951. 13,140 gross tons; 528 feet long; 69 feet wide. Sulzer diesels, twin screw. Service speed 18 knots. 672 passengers (136 first-class, 304 tourist-class, 232 third-class).]

AFRICA. Within a year of building the 1951 trio, Lloyd Triestino added two fine motor liners for its east and south African service. The *Africa,* shown here at Trieste, ***below,*** with the *Vulcania* at dock as well, entered service in February 1952, the identical *Europa* during October. Similar to the *Australia* class, they, too, had a balance between passengers and freight, the latter having five holds, including one that was refrigerated. The passenger accommodations were done in fine Italian contemporary and included such amenities as complete air-conditioning, lido decks with tiled pools and colorful umbrella-topped tables, and private bathrooms in every first-class cabin and lots of semi-private facilities in the less expensive tourist-class rooms. Making monthly departures from Italy, the *Africa* and *Europa* sailed from Trieste, Venice, and Brindisi to Port Said, Suez, Aden, Mogadishu, Mombasa, Dar-es-Salaam, Beira, Durban, and Capetown. Port Elizabeth and East London were included on the homeward trips. [Built by Cantieri Riuniti dell'Adriatico, Monfalcone, Italy, 1952. 11,434 gross tons; 523 feet long; 68 feet wide. Fiat diesels, twin screw. Service speed 19½ knots. 446 passengers (148 first-class, 298 tourist-class).]

VICTORIA. To revive the famed prewar service to India and the Far East, near duplicates of the *Africa* and *Europa* were created: the twin sisters *Asia* and *Victoria* (which is seen here being launched at Monfalcone on September 18, 1951, ***above***). Completed in the spring of 1953, they, too, made monthly sailings from Italy, departing from Genoa and Naples for Port Said, Suez, Aden, Karachi, Bombay, Colombo, Singapore, and Hong Kong. [Built by Cantieri Riuniti dell'Adriatico, Monfalcone, Italy, 1953. 11,693 gross tons; 522 feet long; 68 feet wide. Fiat diesels, twin screw. Service speed 19½ knots. 431 passengers (290 first-class, 141 tourist-class).]

With her sleek, handsome lines quite evident in this image, ***opposite, top,*** the *Victoria* has been the last survivor of these postwar Lloyd Triestino combination liners. After the others were sold off or scrapped in the 1970s, she was sold in 1978 to Youth-With-A-Mission Group and became the *Anastasis,* a roving, worldwide missionary ship. She had a life-extending refit at Cadiz in Spain in 2004.

DONIZETTI. In 1963, there was something of a reshuffling in the Finmare-controlled passenger fleet. As the brand-new *Guglielmo Marconi* and *Galileo Galilei* were coming into Australian service for Lloyd Triestino, the three sisters on that trade, the *Australia, Neptunia,* and *Oceania,* were transferred to the Italian Line, which was upgrading its liner services to the west coast of South America. The three ships were refitted, with their accommodations restyled for only two classes—first and tourist—and renamed *Donizetti* (seen here, ***opposite, bottom***), *Rossini,* and *Verdi*—the so-called "Three Musicians." Hereafter, they ran a lengthy, port-filled service from Genoa, Cannes, Barcelona, and Lisbon to La Guaira, Curacao, Cartagena, and Cristobal in the Caribbean. Then, after transiting the Panama Canal, they called at South American west coast ports: Buenaventura, Guayaquil, Callao, Arica, and Valparaiso. The thirty-day voyage from Genoa to Valparaiso was, for example, priced at $600 in first class and $450 in tourist class. Later, when Italian Line decided to phase out its passenger operations in the mid-1970s, these three ships were retired. In 1976, each of them went to Italian shipbreakers. [Built by Cantieri Riuniti dell'Adriatico, Trieste, Italy, 1951. 13,226 gross tons; 528 feet long; 69 feet wide. Sulzer diesels, twin screw. Service speed 17½ knots. 600 passengers (160 first-class, 440 tourist-class).]

MESSAPIA. Another member of the government's Finmare Group was the Adriatica Line, which specialized in intra-Mediterranean service. Among its newest and finest postwar passenger ships, the sisters *Enotria* and *Messapia* (seen here arriving at Venice, ***above***) were created especially for service to Greece, Cyprus, and Israel. While the *Enotria* was based from Genoa and Naples, the *Messapia* sailed from Trieste, Venice, and Brindisi. [Built by Cantieri Navale di Taranto, Taranto, Italy, 1952. 5,207 gross tons; 383 feet long; 54 feet wide. Fiat diesels, twin screw. Service speed 16 knots. 242 passengers (76 first-class, 44 second-class, 162 third-class).]

ROMA. After World War II, emigration from Italy, as well as other parts of Europe, was booming. Millions were seeking new and better lives elsewhere: North, Central, and South America as well as Australia. Italian shipowners saw great potential at the time, and created ships specially designed for the budget, low-fare trades. Naples-based Flotta Lauro took, among other ships, two former wartime "baby flattops" and had them gutted and rebuilt in 1950 as the passenger liners *Roma* and *Sydney*. Designed especially for the Italy-Australia run, their two-class quarters included complete air-conditioning, outdoor pools and even an open-air cinema. In this view, ***opposite, top,*** dated April 16, 1957, the *Roma* is making an unusual call at Valletta on Malta to off-load a large shipment of South African apples and oranges. She had been specially rerouted on her homeward journey from Sydney and Melbourne to Naples and Genoa via Durban and Capetown. She was also delivering 150 Maltese emigrants who were unhappy with their new lives in Australia. [Built by Seattle-Tacoma Shipbuilding Corporation, Tacoma, Washington, 1946. 14,687 gross tons; 492 feet long; 69 feet wide. Steam turbines, single screw. Service speed 17 knots. 1,113 passengers (119 first-class, 994 tourist-class).]

ACHILLE LAURO. To strengthen its still-busy Australian trade, Flotta Lauro bought two large Dutch liners, the *Oranje* and *Willem Ruys,* and had them totally rebuilt as modern passenger ships, the *Angelina Lauro* and *Achille Lauro,* ***opposite, bottom,*** respectively. Both ships were introduced in 1966 and soon used on an expanded around-the-world service. Used mostly as cruise ships by the 1970s, the *Angelina Lauro* burned in the Caribbean in March 1979 and later sank while being towed to Far Eastern ship-breakers, while the *Achille Lauro,* perhaps best remembered for her headline-making hijacking in October 1985, burned and sank off east Africa in late December 1994. [Built by De Schelde Shipyard, Flushing, Netherlands, 1939–47. 23,629 gross tons in 1966. 631 feet long; 82 feet wide. Sulzer diesels, twin screw. Service speed 22 knots. 1,652 passengers after 1966 (152 first-class, approximately 1,500 tourist-class).]

ROMA
NAPOLI

ACHILLE LAURO

PACE. Using the former American passenger ship *Cuba,* which was built for Peninsular & Occidental Steamship Company's Tampa–Havana service, Italian shipowners Ignazio Messina & Company bought her after World War II and pressed her into Mediterranean service as the *Pace,* ***above.*** She ran regular service to Egypt and Lebanon, sailing from Genoa via Marseilles, Naples, and Malta to Alexandria and Beirut, and then returning to Genoa via Candia, Messina, Naples, and Marseilles. The four-day voyage from Genoa to Alexandria was priced in the 1950s at $140 for a first-class double to $73 in a ten-berth dormitory in third class. She also made trips to Haifa, several east African ports, and went on several immigrant voyages to Central and South America. [Built by William Cramp & Sons Ship & Engine Building Company, Philadelphia, Pennsylvania, 1921. 4,013 gross tons; 325 feet long; 57 feet wide. Steam triple expansion engines, twin screw. Service speed 17 knots. Approximately 500 passengers in first- and third-class.]

HOMERIC. While not precisely an Italian company, the multinational Home Lines, with Italian, Greek, Swiss, Swedish, and even American partners, used Genoa as an operational base. The company specialized in taking secondhand liners and refitting them for further service, mostly on the North Atlantic to either New York or the Canadian ports of Montreal and Quebec City. Beginning in 1955, its flagship was the *Homeric,* ***below,*** which had been the popular American liner *Mariposa* of the 1930s. For Home Lines, she sailed for about nine months of the year between Cuxhaven (Hamburg), Le Havre, Southampton, Quebec, and Montreal; for the remainder, she ran one-class, wintertime cruises from New York to the Caribbean. [Built by Bethlehem Steel Company, Quincy, Massachusetts, 1931. 24,907 gross tons; 638 feet long; 79 feet wide. Steam turbines, twin screw. Service speed 20 knots. 1,243 passengers (147 first-class, 1,096 tourist-class).]

VENEZUELA. Another Italian shipowner that was largely interested in the big postwar immigrant and low-fare trades was the Grimaldi-Siosa Lines. It, too, bought older, secondhand passenger ships and rebuilt them for further service, usually with greatly expanded accommodations. The *Venezuela,* the company flagship in the late 1950s, had been the prewar *De Grasse* of the French Line. Sunk and then salvaged during the war, she was restored and used in further French service until sold, in 1953, to Canadian Pacific, who sailed her to Canada from Liverpool as the *Empress of Australia.* Grimaldi-Siosa bought her in 1956 and placed her in Central American service: Naples, Genoa, Cannes, and Barcelona to Tenerife and then across to Caribbean waters: Guadeloupe, Martinique, La Guaira, and Trinidad. She went aground at Cannes in March 1962, was badly damaged, and is seen here subsequently laid-up at Genoa before being sold for demolition, ***above.*** [Built by Cammell Laird & Company Limited, Birkenhead, England, 1924. 18,769 gross tons; 597 feet long; 71 feet wide. Steam turbines, twin screw. Service speed 18 knots. 1,480 passengers (180 first-class, 500 tourist-cabin-class, 800 tourist-minimum-class).]

FRANCA C. The Genoa-based Costa Line entered the passenger ship business in 1948 and gradually built up one of the world's largest and most modern fleets. In the beginning, it, too, relied on second-hand ships, such as the former freighter *Medina,* built just as World War I started, and rebuilt as the passenger ship *Roma* in the late 1940s. Costa bought her in 1952 and renamed her *Franca C.,* then used her in the Central and South American immigrant trades (as seen here, ***below***) before converting her in 1959 to a very fine single-class cruise ship. She was a pioneer winter Caribbean cruise ship based at the then-infant port of Miami in the early 1960s, offered the very first air-sea package cruise-tour in 1968. [Built by Newport News Shipbuilding & Dry Dock Company, Newport News, Virginia, 1914. 6,549 gross tons in 1959. 428 feet long; 55 feet wide. Fiat diesel, single screw. Service speed 15½ knots. 354 all-first-class passengers.]

The Costa Line used some of the best examples of contemporary Italian decor for its passenger ships. Here we see the restaurant aboard the *Franca C,* ***above.***

FEDERICO C. Within ten years of entering the passenger ship trades and using rebuilt, secondhand ships, the Costa Line built its first large liner, the *Federico C.* She followed the general design style of the Italian Line's *Giulio Cesare* (1951) and the *Andrea Doria* (1952), and with a basic external format that continued with ships such as Adriatica Line's *Ausonia* (1957) and *Leonardo da Vinci* (1960). For a time, the *Federico C,* seen here at Genoa, ***opposite, bottom,*** on the left with the *Augustus* in the center and the *Cristoforo Colombo* to the right, was considered the finest Italian liner on the run from Genoa, Cannes, Barcelona, and Lisbon to Rio de Janeiro, Santos, Montevideo, and Buenos Aires. [Built by Ansaldo Shipyard, Genoa, Italy, 1958. 20,416 gross tons; 606 feet long; 79 feet wide. Steam turbines, twin screw. Service speed 21 knots. 1,279 passengers (243 first-class, 300 cabin-class, 736 tourist-class).]

Noted maritime author Laurence Dunn wrote of the *Federico C* in 1961, "Exceptional care was paid to the design and decor of accommodations and public rooms, which are in contemporary Italian style with restrained use of colors. And second class is but very little short of first-class standards." In this view, we see a first-class bedroom with adjoining sitting room, ***above.***

ENRICO C. Even subsequent secondhand liner tonnage was rebuilt and upgraded to meet the high Costa Line standards. Here we see the tourist-class pool, ***below,*** done in a typically unusual shape by the Italians, aboard the modernized *Enrico C.* She joined the Costa fleet in 1965, having sailed previously as the *Provence* for France's Transports Maritimes. [Built by Swan, Hunter & Wigham Richardson Limited, Newcastle, England, 1950. 13,607 gross tons; 580 feet long; 73 feet wide. Steam turbines, twin screw. Service speed 18 knots. 1,198 passengers (218 first-class, 980 tourist-class).]

FAIRSEA. Sitmar Line was another important postwar Italian passenger line interested in the immigrant and budget tourist markets. It, too, took older tonnage and rebuilt them for all-tourist-class service. Its *Fairsea* had an interesting background—intended to be the combination passenger-cargo liner *Rio de la Plata* for New York-based Moore-McCormack Lines in 1941, she was instead completed for war duties as the small British aircraft carrier *Charger.* Idle in the late 1940s, she was sold to Sitmar, gutted, and thoroughly rebuilt in 1948–49. As the *Fairsea,* ***above,*** she sailed in around-the-world service: From Southampton to Suez, Aden, Fremantle, Melbourne, Sydney, Auckland, Papeete, Balboa, Cristobal, Curacao, Lisbon, and back to Southampton. To suit her low rates, all but ten of her cabins were without private bathroom facilities. In 1969, a fire disabled the *Fairsea,* after which she was towed to Italy to be broken-up. [Built by Sun Shipbuilding & Dry Dock Company, Chester, Pennsylvania, 1941. 13,432 gross tons; 492 feet long; 69 feet wide. Doxford diesel, single screw. Service speed 16 knots. 1,460 all-tourist-class passengers.]

AURELIA. Another postwar Italian conversion for the budget liner trades was the *Aurelia,* owned by the Genoa-based Cogedar Line. Having been the German combination ship *Huascaran* and later Canadian Pacific's *Beaverbrae,* she, too, was used in the very lucrative Australian trade, from Italian as well as North European ports, and also made occasional charter sailings, such as summer crossings on the North Atlantic between Southampton, Le Havre, and New York with teachers, students, and their chaperones. We see her here, in a photograph dated June 9, 1962, at Manhattan's Pier 84, ***below.*** [Built by Blohm & Voss Shipbuilders, Hamburg, Germany, 1939. 10,480 gross tons; 487 feet long; 60 feet wide. Diesel-electric, single screw. Service speed 17 knots. 1,124 all-tourist-class passengers.]

MARCONI. Two of the last survivors of the big Italian passenger fleet of the 1950s and 1960s were the Lloyd Triestino sister ships *Guglielmo Marconi* and *Galileo Galilei*. Big, fast, and luxurious, they were built for the final heyday of the Italy-Australia trade. By the late 1970s, however, they sought profits elsewhere, mostly in the cruise trades. Prodded by the powerful Italian maritime unions, the *Marconi* was used for a short-lived cruise service from New York to the Caribbean in 1978–79 under the banner Italian Line Cruises International. Seen here on her inaugural visit to New York in December 1978, ***above,*** she was a misplaced attempt to continue the services of the original Italian Line. In 1983, both ships, by then struggling, were sold. The *Marconi* became Costa's greatly rebuilt *Costa Riviera* (with a short stint on charter as the *American Pioneer*) before being scrapped in India in 2002 under the final name *Liberty*. The *Galileo* went in 1983 to the Greek-owned Chandris-Celebrity Cruises, sailing first under her original name, and, after a thorough rebuilding in 1990, as the *Meridian* before being sold in 1997 to become the Singapore-owned *Sun Vista*. The former *Galileo* burned and then sank off Malaysia in May 1999. [Built by Cantieri Riuniti dell'Adriatico, Monfalcone, Italy, 1963. 27,900 gross tons; 702 feet long; 94 feet wide. Steam turbines, twin screw. Service speed 24 knots. 1,750 passengers as built (156 first-class, 1,594 tourist-class).]

CHAPTER SEVEN

Last of the Fleet: The End of a Grand Era

"They were all great ships, grand ladies. It was a luxurious time, a different world in many ways. It is now gone, totally vanished ... I feel nostalgic." So commented Rosalbo Lottero, who served aboard the passenger ships of the Italian Line for fourteen years. Known professionally as "Bino," he was part of an orchestra that traveled all around Europe in the early 1960s when an advertisement in a Genoa newspaper changed his career and his life. "The Italian Line offered jobs for show-business types with multilingual abilities," he recollected. "There were 300 applicants. I was one of the ten to be selected."

In 1996, while cruise director on a more current Italian ship, the *Monterey,* Bino recalled what he dubbed "the golden days." In 1963, his first posting was to the *Cristoforo Colombo,* then sailing on the "express run" between Naples, Genoa, Cannes, Gibraltar, and New York. "I was the 'Director of Social Activities'—[there was no] cruise director in those days—who organized games and performances in the ship's three classes. We had separate orchestras, but we rotated the performers. Of course, we paid lots of attention to first class and a little less to cabin class. At the time, we also had closed-circuit television in the lounges and each day we broadcast the news. Actually, it was telex news we received from AP [Associated Press] and UPI [United Press International]."

"First class was very luxurious, very sophisticated," he remembered. "We had the likes of Maria Callas, Elizabeth Taylor, the Rockefellers. The King of Arabia traveled with us and used to reserve an entire deck for his many wives, ministers, servants, and bodyguards. And, of course, we had all the Italian celebrities: Sophia Loren, Marcello Mastroanni, Renata Tebaldi, Silvana Mangano, Virna Lisi, Monica Vitti, and Gina Lollobrigida. And we had all the cardinals and the bishops and their entourages from the Roman church. Toward the end, we had the widowed Duchess of Windsor. She came to dinner each evening, but sometimes she was very confused. She was very old and very frail. Cabin class was more for tourists, the traveling professional people: doctors, lawyers, teachers, technicians. In tourist class, we still had many, many Italian immigrants, but it was not exactly like earlier times, say the 1920s and '30s. In the '60s, immigrants were far more knowledgeable. They were not going to the 'unknown,' but were helped by family and friends already in America. Altogether, our biggest and most serious competitors were the two American liners, the *Independence* and *Constitution.*"

Bino later served aboard the final Italian Line passenger ships, the *Leonardo da Vinci* and the twin sisters *Michelangelo* and *Raffaello.* But by the early 1970s, the sole profit of these big Italian ocean liners became purely prestige. "Our business was declining. The jumbo jet did us in," said a saddened Lottero. "The airlines took all the business, even the immigrants. Now, only seven hours and they could be in America! We tried more and more cruises. But we continued too long. The government liked the prestige of these ships, much like in Mussolini's time in the 1930s, and was even willing to pay the increasing subsidies. And there were 20,000 employees, mostly from Genoa and Naples, to be considered. But the Italian Line had always been too big, too fat. It was all politics. There were ten managers and twenty assistant managers, for example, for each department at the Genoa home office. There were four men at each reservation phone and they rotated calls. The end began in 1975, when the *Michelangelo* and *Raffaello* were retired. Other ships then followed. I was aboard the very last Italian crossing. We sailed from Port Everglades, Florida to Genoa aboard the *Leonardo da Vinci.* The date was March 1978. But even now, some twenty years later, I miss those old liners, those grand ladies. It was a great era."

LEONARDO DA VINCI. Within days of the sinking of the *Andrea Doria,* the Italian Line sought to restore passenger and staff morale, reestablish its credibility as a prime transatlantic liner company, and bolster national prestige. From the company's Genoa headquarters came news of the building order for a larger, more luxurious liner for the express run to New York. She would be Italy's biggest and most expensive liner to date and, as part of a lavish and extensive promotion, an eighteen-foot-long model of the ship, created a year before the actual ship's completion, was sent on tour. Seen here in the Galleria Vittorio Emanuele in Milan, ***opposite,*** it was also on show in New York City's Grand Central Station in December 1959. An advertisement read, "Six months away to the finest Italian liner yet!" The ship itself, already the pride of Genoa, had been launched a year before, on December 7, 1958, and was named *Leonardo da Vinci* by the wife of the president of Italy. [Built by Ansaldo Shipyards, Genoa, Italy, 1960. 33,340 gross tons; 761 feet long; 92 feet wide. Steam turbines, twin screw. Service speed 23 knots. 1,326 passengers (413 first-class, 342 cabin-class, 571 tourist-class).]

"The *Leonardo da Vinci,* ***above,*** was the Italian government's immediate response to the sinking of the *Andrea Doria,*" noted Der Scutt. "Her exterior pursued the simplicity and elegance of the *Doria.* While the *da Vinci* was longer, the designers were still able to integrate the rounded bridge front (superstructure) while adhering to the streamlined stepping of the aft decks. Later, I preferred the black hull to a white one, which I felt made the ship appear more distinctive." The *da Vinci,* immediately appraised as one of the handsomest liners of her time, was an obvious descendant of the *Andrea Doria* and *Cristoforo Colombo.* Sleek and more rounded, she had some noted changes, such as the elimination of the aft cargo spaces, which were better used as expanded lido and pool areas for her three classes. Dressed in colorful flags, the new Italian Line broke the quiet mood of a warm Saturday morning in New York in July 1960 when she arrived for the first time. Italian Line press material told of the ship's many fine and innovative qualities and that she would be revolutionary: she was designed with an eye toward the future and most likely would be converted to nuclear power by as early as 1965.

LEONARDO DA VINCI

LEONARDO

For five years, until 1965, the *Leonardo da Vinci,* seen here at Genoa, ***opposite, top,*** and the *Cristoforo Colombo* (left) maintained the Italy–New York express, making regular three-week round-trip voyages between Naples, Genoa, Cannes, Gibraltar, and Manhattan's Pier 84. Peak summer season fares began at $390 in first class, $300 in cabin class, and $236 in tourist class. The *da Vinci* offered six swimming pools, very modern public rooms, and private facilities in 80 percent of her cabins.

Scutt added further comment on the design of the new *da Vinci.* "It was interesting to note that the *Leonardo da Vinci*'s main mast was a symbol of high-tech navigational safety with its multi-layered radar platforms, lookout, and so forth. This was probably a response to the sinking of the *Andrea Doria.*"

The *da Vinci* did have one noted blemish, however—stability problems. Some 3,000 tons of iron had to be added to her double bottom. This, of course, made her heavier than planned, and the weight caused added drag and therefore extra fuel consumption. "I recall going below decks and seeing the pig iron that was added for greater stability," remembered Captain Ed Squire. "And I recall seeing the area that was to be used for the installation of a nuclear reactor." Ultimately, the beautiful *da Vinci* was far less of a financial success than her Italian designers, builders, and owners had expected.

In her early years, the *Leonardo da Vinci* made an annual, long, luxurious, extended cruise around the Mediterranean. In this image taken on February 15, 1963, ***opposite, bottom,*** she departed from New York on a fifty-one-day itinerary, with her capacity especially reduced to a 600-person all-first class, calling at Lisbon, Palma, Palermo, Crete, Alexandria, Larnaca, Beirut, Haifa, Istanbul, Yalta, Varna, Piraeus, Dubrovnik, Messina, Naples, Genoa, Cannes, Barcelona, Casablanca, and Tenerife. Fares began at $1,495, or just under $30 per person per day.

The *Leonardo da Vinci* was considered one of the most modern and most beautifully decorated liners of the 1960s. In these views, we see the first-class main lounge, ***above,*** and a bar-lounge in tourist class, ***below.***

"The Italian set standards in the 1950s and '60s," commented Charles Howland. "It is interesting to note, however, that the ships of Costa Line are some of the most innovative ships sailing today. In an ironic way, then, the Italians are still setting the standard in big ship design." Here is the cabin-class lido and pool area aboard the *da Vinci* (***above***).

"Cunard was the only serious rival to the Italians in the 1950s and early '60s," remarked Scutt. "France, for example, placed all efforts in one ship, namely the *France,* whereas the Italian postwar newbuilds were very aggressive. The image of Italian postwar liners varied considerably with each ship. There seemed to be an ever-increasing desire to enhance and improve each ship. The Italian liners possessed a kind of general appeal with their innovative exterior design characteristics and intimate comfortable interiors, whereas Cunard's 'assembly line' of ships was less dramatic than those of the Italians. Even the Costa ships had nifty, sleek, nautical curves—vivacious, like the Italian women. Cunard's answer was the 'stately matron.'" The Italian Line flagship is seen here outbound on another Atlantic crossing as she passes under the new Verrazano Narrows Bridge in New York City, ***opposite, top.*** The year is 1965.

The *Leonardo da Vinci* actually closed out Italian Line's transatlantic passenger service from New York in June 1976. She was reactivated the following year, but for the newly created (thanks to the Italian unions) Italian Line Cruises International. Managed, in fact, by the Costa Line, she was used mostly in short, three- and four-day cruises between Port Everglades, Florida, and the Bahamas. She proved to be an expensive, money-losing ship, however, and was quickly back in Italy and laid-up at La Spezia. There were rumors that she would see further life as a luxury cruise ship, as a floating hotel and even as a moored casino in the River Thames, but nothing came to pass. On July 4, 1980, while empty and anchored at La Spezia, she mysteriously caught fire, burned for four days, and then capsized, ***opposite, bottom.*** Later pumped out and righted, she was scrapped locally in 1982.

MICHELANGELO

ARTISTS ON SEA: *MICHELANGELO* AND *RAFFAELLO*. Soon after the *Leonardo da Vinci* was commissioned in the spring of 1960, Italian unions—the shipyard workers, dockers, and the seamen—began prodding the government to build additional Atlantic liners. In reality, it was becoming too late for such ships. The jets were showing their paces and, by 1963, had secured no less than 95 percent of the North Atlantic passenger business. The government, as well as the Italian Line directors, persisted, and ordered no less than two powerful and lavish 45,000-ton super liners for the express run between Naples, Genoa, and New York. The first of the $120 million pair was the *Michelangelo*, ***opposite,*** which came from the Ansaldo yard at Genoa and was launched on September 16, 1962. [Built by Ansaldo Shipyards, Genoa, Italy, 1965. 45,911 gross tons; 902 feet long; 102 feet wide. Steam turbines, twin screw. Service speed 26.5 knots. 1,775 passengers (535 first-class, 550 cabin-class, 690 tourist-class).]

Sensibly, the second super ship, the *Raffaello*, ***above,*** was built on the Adriatic, at Monfalcone. She was launched on March 24, 1963. There were some final changes made to the twin liners as well. Both were to have traditional Italian Line black hulls, but they were completed with all-white hulls to convey a more cruise-like feel. By 1966, both the *Leonardo da Vinci* and *Cristoforo Colombo* were changed to white as well. [Built by Cantieri Riuniti dell'Adriatico, Monfalcone, Italy, 1965. 45,933 gross tons; 902 feet long; 102 feet wide. Steam turbines, twin screw. Service speed 26.5 knots. 1,775 passengers (535 first-class, 550 cabin-class, 690 tourist-class).]

As the *Raffaello* was being fitted out in the spring of 1965, as seen here in this photo at Monfalcone, ***above,*** the transatlantic liner trade was in its twilight. But there was a burst of new ship construction even beyond the ambitious two Italians. The French, for example, added the 66,000-ton *France* in 1962, Canadian Pacific introduced their new flagship, the 27,000-ton *Empress of Canada,* the year before, and Israel's Zim Lines commissioned their 25,000-ton *Shalom* in 1964.

Prior to the *Michelangelo*'s maiden sailing from Genoa on May 12, 1965, Giuseppe Cardinal Siri, who had blessed the liner at her launching, toured the finished ship, ***below.*** He baptized almost all of the Genoa-built liners in the 1950s and '60s. To the right of the Cardinal is Captain Mario Crepaz, commodore commander of the Italian Line fleet at the time.

"It was interesting to note that the bridge command centers on each ship were like hospital operating rooms—spotless with shiny linoleum floors and clean, modern nautical equipment," noted Scutt. "One could eat off the floors."

Long, sleek, and white, the splendid appearances of the two new Italian liners seemed to be dominated by their twin funnels done in lattice caging and capped with long exhaust sweeps, ***above.*** "The *Michelangelo* and her sister had nice lines," commented ocean liner collector Richard Romano, "but I always felt that the birdcage funnels looked unfinished." Captain Ed Squire added, "They were magnificent ships, but built too late for the Atlantic trade. They had great design and I especially admired the originality of their unusual, lattice-work funnels, but which always reminded me of upside-down New York City trash barrels."

"Even though the Italians were aware that transportation on Atlantic liners was waning, they nevertheless continued their aggressive pursuit of ocean liner dominance," said Scutt. "The government's mandate for the building of these last two ships stated that they would have to be 'ideal passenger carriers of today and tomorrow.' The planning design had to go beyond merely working out something new and different. The designers had to strive for unprecedented perfection in all respects."

"As such, the exteriors of these two ships [the *Michelangelo* is seen here, ***below,*** arriving in New York for the first time in May 1965] were exquisitely smooth and pristine in character, perhaps reflecting the simple, very modern interiors," added Scutt. "Of special interest, the sheer white hulls, almost void of portholes, epitomized the modern sleekness. In the design of these two ships, the bridge front was now more vertical and less rounded, which enhanced the image of these vessels as being fast, efficient, and superior."

The Italian Line's publicity and promotions department planned a glorious, commemorative occasion. The *Michelangelo* joined the *Raffaello* (seen on the right, ***above***) when she arrived in New York for the first time in July 1965. The two new, gleaming Italian superships created a most impressive picture as they were berthed at Pier 90, the former Cunard Line terminal at the foot of West 50th Street and to which the Italian Line had relocated from Pier 84 in 1964. In this scene, the liner *United States* is at the far left, while the *Queen Mary* is in mid-river, about to dock.

"The last of the Italian liners, the *da Vinci,* the *Michelangelo,* and the *Raffaello,* became classics but only later with me," Frank Trumbour recalled. "When they were new, the *Michelangelo* and *Raffaello* were simply too contemporary for my taste. I only began to appreciate their exterior beauty in recent years. The *da Vinci* was too modern to a degree, but ran close to the earlier *Doria* and *Colombo*. She looked like them, but obviously a little more modern and did not have quite as much exterior grace as they did."

The Italian liners of the 1950s and '60s were noted for their rolling and pitching at sea. "Even the *Leonardo da Vinci* had to add thousands of tons of ballast soon after completion," remembered Scutt. "The *Andrea Doria*'s instability was well known, and both the *Michelangelo* and *Raffaello,* ***opposite, top,*** contributed to their share of spilled wine." The worst occasion for the *Michelangelo* came during a westbound crossing in April 1966. The aluminum forestructure of the ship crumbled under the weight of an enormous wave, and it was only through good fortune that the entire bridge did not collapse as well. The liner arrived in New York, delayed and wounded, with canvas coverings over her forward decks. Temporarily repaired at Pier 90 by work barges and floating cranes, she returned to Genoa to have her support structure reinforced with stronger steel.

To offset their losses on the Atlantic run, where they were often filled only to 50 percent capacity, both the *Michelangelo* (seen here at New York, ***opposite, bottom***) and the *Raffaello* were increasingly sent on lucrative, one-class cruises: New York to the Caribbean, to Rio for Carnival, and, on occasion, from Genoa around the Mediterranean, to west Africa, and on at least one occasion northward to Scandinavia.

RAFFAELLO
1

The *Michelangelo* and *Raffaello* continued the tradition of fine, contemporary interior decor as seen in these views of the first-class bar aboard the *Raffaello*, ***opposite, top,*** and the first-class dining room, ***opposite, bottom,*** and main lounge on the *Michelangelo*, ***above.*** These days, there is tremendous nostalgic interest and appeal in the Italian liners. "I think that the postwar liners are very popular with the ship-buff community because many can remember them vividly and so there is this tangible link," explained Frank Trumbour. "With a very few other exceptions, they continued on the Atlantic for a fairly long time. So again, people not only recall their existence, but their arrivals and departures, especially at New York."

Richard Faber added, "The Italian Line has a strong image, even some twenty-five years after the final crossing to Naples and Genoa. Those final liners represent the Mediterranean, romance—a sort of eternal sunshine." In a very rare occasion, ***below,*** the last Italian Line super ships, the *Michelangelo* (foreground) and the *Raffaello*, sail together from New York on September 22, 1972. By now, the ships were losing millions and there were rumors of placing the *Raffaello* in Italy–South America service.

LAST CALL. The final gathering of the last three Italian Line passenger ships at New York came in January 1969, ***opposite, top.*** The *Leonardo da Vinci* is at Pier 92 on the left, the *Michelangelo* in the middle at Pier 90, and the *Raffaello* on the right as seen in this view from a departing Moran tug. Deep in debt, struggling for passengers, and costing a small fortune to the Italian government in operating subsidies, the two larger liners were withdrawn from service in 1975—the *Raffaello* in April and the *Michelangelo* that July. Laid up at La Spezia, the rumors of their next roles ran rampant—floating cancer research clinics, moored housing in Brazil, restored cruise liners for Home Lines and Norwegian Caribbean Lines, and combination hotel-conference centers in the Mediterranean. In the end, they were sold to the Iranian government in 1977 for use as military barracks—the *Michelangelo* at Bandar Abbas, the *Raffaello* at Bushire. There, they soon fell into neglected, deplorable condition: rat-infested, rusting, and fading under the relentless Middle Eastern sun. Even the Italian advisory crews had deserted them. The *Raffaello* was destroyed in February 1983 during an Iraqi air attack, her remains sunk in harbor waters. The *Michelangelo* was sold for $1 million in 1991 to Pakistani scrappers. It took six months to demolish her.

COSTA FORTUNA. The great art of shipbuilding was revived at Genoa by the summer of 2003, when the 105,000-ton *Costa Fortuna,* ***opposite, bottom,*** was completed by the former Ansaldo yards at nearby Sestri-Ponente. Owned by the Genoa-based Costa Cruises, she ranked at the time as the largest liner to date built in Italy. Easily surpassing the likes of the 51,000-ton *Rex* and the 45,000-ton *Michelangelo* and *Raffaello,* her decorative theme throughout is thoughtfully and historically linked to those great, record-breaking liners of the past. The ship's Grand Atrium is depicted like the ocean, with twenty-six models of Costa Line passenger ships suspended upside-down from the painted ceiling. The theme is also represented by the *Rex* Theatre, *Michelangelo* and *Raffaello* restaurants, *Roma* Bar, *Conte Verde* Ballroom, *Conte Grande* Tavernetta, and the *Neptunia* Casino. Paolo Piccione, a Genoa-based marine designer and architect, praised the new liner, declaring the *Costa Fortuna,* "a feast for the ocean liner enthusiast and a proud tribute to those great passenger ships of the past."

With Costa being the biggest cruise operator in Europe in a rapidly expanding market, the *Fortuna*'s record was predictably surpassed within a year by the slightly larger *Costa Magica.* In 2006, both will be eclipsed by the 112,000-ton, 3,200-bed *Costa Concordia.* Meanwhile, as of late 2004, the Fincantieri shipyard is said to be under consideration for the construction of a 180,000-ton, 4,500-passenger ultra-cruise ship dubbed the "Pinnacle Project." To be built for Carnival, the parent of Costa and many other cruise lines, it is most likely that such a ship would be assigned to their Princess Cruises division. Thus, while not only building the largest Italian liners of all time, indeed successors to the *Andrea Doria,* Italy is building the world's largest passenger ships as well. [Built by Fincantieri, Genoa, Italy, 2003. 105,000 tons; 890 feet long; 124 feet wide. Diesels, twin screw. Service speed 20 knots. 2,720 cruise passengers.]

POSTSCRIPT. The Italian Line and, in particular, the *Andrea Doria,* continues to capture our imaginations. In July 2004, there was a festive gala at the port of Genoa—a centuries-old maritime center that welcomed many ships, including most of the grand Italian liners mentioned in these pages. The celebration marked the opening of the new Museum of the Seas, located in the harborside Galata Building, built to remind us of that northern Italian seaport's great and diverse seafaring heritage.

The five-story building housed a lavish exhibit, co-sponsored by Costa Cruises and Fincantieri, the noted shipbuilder that runs the nearby Ansaldo yard, where ships such as the *Andrea Doria* were constructed some fifty years ago. The exhibit began with Columbus's voyages of discovery and spanned the centuries to the modern era of ocean liners. For ocean-liner buffs, there was items of special interest: the bell and other artifacts from the 1932-built *Rex,* large-scale models of ships including the *Queen Elizabeth, Federico C,* and *Eugenio C,* and—poignantly—the bust of Andrea Doria from his namesake ship. Expectedly, there was considerable material from the Italian Line from the era of their grand liners. The exhibit, to which the Ocean Liner Council in New York contributed, drew tens of thousands of eager ship enthusiasts to Genoa. For many, a visit was in itself a journey of rich nostalgia.

Happily—judging from events such as these, as well as the popularity of ship-themed books and lectures—it appears that there is still a deep interest in legendary liners like the *Andrea Doria.* Though many are no longer sailing, they will undoubtedly live on in our memories.

ITALIAN
LINE
M

C
COSTA FORTUNA

Bibliography

Bonsor, N. R. P. *North Atlantic Seaway*. Prescot, Lancashire: T. Stephenson & Sons Limited, 1955.

Braynard, Frank O. *Lives of the Liners*. New York: Cornell Maritime Press, 1947.

Braynard, Frank O. & Miller, William H. *Fifty Famous Liners*, Vols. 1–3. Cambridge, England: Patrick Stephens Limited, 1982–87.

Devol, George, ed. *Ocean & Cruise News*. Stamford, Connecticut: World Ocean & Cruise Society, 1980–2003.

Dunn, Laurence. *Passenger Liners*. Southampton, England: Adlard Coles Limited, 1961.

Eisele, Peter & William Rau, eds. *Steamboat Bill*. New York: Steamship Historical Society of America Inc., 1965–2003.

Eliseo, Maurizio. *Rex*. Parma, Italy: Ermanno Albertelli Editore, 1992.

Haws, Duncan. *Merchant Fleets: Italia 1881–2001*. Pembroke, Great Britain. 2001.

Kludas, Arnold. *Great Passenger Ships of the World, Vols. 1–5*. Cambridge, England: Patrick Stephens Limited, 1972–76.

Miller, William H. *Passenger Liners Italian Style*. London: Carmania Press Ltd., 1996.

———. *Picture History of the Italian Line 1932–1977*. Mineola, New York: Dover Publications Inc., 1999.

Official Steamship Guide. New York: Transportation Guides Inc., 1937–63.

Index of Ships

Many of the ships mentioned in this book have carried different names during their careers. With a few exceptions, only the name most relevant to the text is reflected in this index.